THE POWER OF PRAYER

IN MODERN ENGLISH WITH INTRODUCTION
AND A STUDY GUIDE

C. H. SPURGEON

GODLIPRESS TEAM

© Copyright 2022 by GodliPress. All rights reserved.

This book is copyright protected. You cannot amend, distribute, sell, use, quote or paraphrase any part, or the content within this book, without the consent of the author or publisher, except in the case of brief quotations embodied in critical articles or reviews.

Scripture quotations are from The ESV® Bible (The Holy Bible, English Standard Version®), copyright © 2001 by Crossway, a publishing ministry of Good News Publishers. Used by permission. All rights reserved.

CONTENTS

Introduction	v
1. PRAYER CERTIFIED OF SUCCESS	1
Jesus Gives Us His Own Authority	4
Jesus Presents Us with a Promise.	12
Jesus Testifies that Prayer Is Heard	16
Study Guide	24
2. THE RAVEN'S CRY	26
You Are Worth More than a Raven	29
Your Cry Is Different to the Raven's	34
Your Prayer Is More Pleasant to God than a Raven's Cry	36
We Are Commanded to Cry to Him, Not the Ravens	38
The Raven's Cry Is Not a Work of Grace	39
You Don't Cry Alone like the Ravens	42
Study Guide	49
3. ORDER AND ARGUMENT IN PRAYER	51
Our Case Must Be Ordered Before God	55
Filling the Mouth with Arguments	63
We Will Have Our Mouths Filled with Praises	74
Study Guide	75
4. PLEADING	77
A Confessing Heart	78
A Pleading Heart	87
An Urgent Heart	94
A Heart that Holds onto God	96
Study Guide	101
5. THE THRONE OF GRACE	103
A Throne	105
Grace	113
Grace Enthroned	119

The Glory of Grace	122
Study Guide	126
6. BRIEF, SILENT PRAYER	127
Nehemiah Prays	130
The Manner of Prayer	133
The Style of Praying	136
Study Guide	148
About C. H. Spurgeon	151

INTRODUCTION

Prayer was one of Charles Spurgeon's favorite topics.

Even among his top-rated books, the topic of prayer was dealt with from several angles. This volume, however, was never intended as a book but is rather a collection of some of his best sermons on the subject. In true Spurgeon style, each aspect dealt with in these pages will challenge, enlighten, and grow you into what he called, "the art of prayer."

Known for his direct, no-nonsense approach behind the pulpit, the essence of his fiery but simple rhetoric makes for the perfect guide or handbook. A simple, direct voice grabs hold of you from the opening statement, and then never lets go until the end. Along the way there will always be something to learn; rarely do readers come away from one of Spurgeon's books without some new form of knowledge.

As classics go, anything with the name 'Spurgeon' attached to it is regarded as a 'must-have' in any well-versed Christian's library. He ranks among the top names in church literature because of his unique style of approaching topics. Whether it's doctrinal issues surrounding baptism, the Holy Spirit, and salvation, or more straightforward subjects like prayer and devotion, you always feel that he is speaking personally to you.

He avoided high, lofty, and academic tones, and instead favored a more conversational attitude, which can be found in the sermons in this book. "The Lord Jesus did not say, 'Feed my giraffes,' but 'Feed my sheep.'" And so, this collection is easy to understand, but not always as easy to digest, because it demands a real, passionate, and devoted response —the same way that he lived his life!

To assist you, you will find the same heart and the same challenge that Spurgeon brought his congregants over 100 years ago but in English you can relate to. Not only that, but a study guide has been designed to guide you to think even further and deeper on his words.

"I would rather teach one man to pray than ten men to preach."

1

PRAYER CERTIFIED OF SUCCESS

"And I tell you, ask, and it will be given to you; seek, and you will find; knock, and it will be opened to you. For everyone who asks receives, and the one who seeks finds, and to the one who knocks it will be opened."
Luke 11:9-10

To find help from a supernatural being in times of distress is instinctive to our human nature. We don't say that those who have not been born again ever offer real spiritual prayer or exercise faith in the living God, but like a child crying in the dark, with painful longing for help from somewhere, they don't even know the heart almost always cries in deep sorrow to some supernatural being for relief. No one has been more ready to pray in times of trouble than those who have laughed at prayer when they were prosperous and had no need of it. The most honest prayers are often those that atheists have offered when they are facing the fear of death.

In one of his writings, Addison describes a man on board a ship, who loudly boasted of his atheism. When a steady storm came up, he fell on his knees and confessed to the minister that he had been an atheist. The sailors who had never heard the word before thought it had been some strange fish, but were more surprised when they saw it was a man, and heard his own words, "that he never believed until that day that there was a God."

One of the more experienced sailors whispered to the ship's officer that it would be good to just throw him overboard, but this was a cruel suggestion, for the poor man was in enough misery already—his atheism had evaporated, and in mortal terror, he cried to God to have mercy on him. Similar incidents have often occurred. They have happened so frequently that we always expect this kind of boastful skepticism to fall apart in the end.

Take away unnatural control from the mind, and we could say that every person, like those on board the ship with Jonah, cry to their God when in trouble. Like birds to their nests, deer to their thickets, so people in agony fly to a superior being for help in times of need. God has given all the creatures He has made different strengths: One can run faster than the wind when it hears the senses danger from the barking of hunting dogs; another one flies on its wings out of reach of being caught; a third animal pushes its enemy down with its horns; and a fourth fights back, tearing its enemy to pieces with tooth and claw.

But He gave very little strength to people, compared with the animals that were placed in Eden, and yet Adam was king over everything because the Lord was His strength. As long as he knew where to look for the source of his power, Adam remained the undisputed monarch of all around him. God sustained His sovereignty over the birds of the air, the animals of the field, and the fish of the sea. By instinct, man turned to God in Paradise. Although people sadly no longer have the same authority as in Eden, there is still the faint memory of what they once were, and of where their strength is still to be found.

Therefore, no matter where a person is, you will find that the one who is in trouble will ask for supernatural help. I believe in the truth of this instinct, and that man prays because there is something in prayer. The same way the Creator gives His creature the power of thirst because water exists to meet its thirst, and when He creates hunger, there is food to meet the appetite. So, when He causes people to pray, it's because prayer has a corresponding blessing connected with it.

The convincing reason for expecting prayer to be effective is because it's established by God. In the Bible, we are commanded to pray again and again. God's ways are not foolish. Can I believe that the infinitely wise God has given me something that is ineffective and nothing more than child's play? Does He ask me to pray if prayer is the same as whistling in the wind or singing to the trees? If there's no answer to prayer, then it's incredible insanity, and God is the author of it, which would be blasphemous to admit. No wise person will continue to pray if you have proved that prayer has no effect with God and never receives an answer. If it's true that the effects of prayer end with the person who prays, then it is only something for idiots and madmen!

I will not enter into any arguments about this matter, but rather focus on the verse, that for me and every other follower of Jesus, is the end of all controversy. Our Savior knew very well that many difficulties would arise in connection with prayer that might throw His disciples off, and so He has counteracted every opposition with an overwhelming assurance.

Read those words, *"And I tell you."* As your Teacher, your Master, your Lord, your Savior, your God, *"I tell you, ask, and it will be given to you; seek, and you will find; knock, and it will be opened to you."*

IN THE VERSE,

Jesus first addresses all difficulties by **giving us the weight of His own authority**, *"And I tell you."* Next, He **presents us with a promise**, *"Ask, and it will be given to you,"* and so on. And then, He **reminds us of an indisputable fact**, *"everyone who asks receives."*

These are three fatal blows for a Christian's doubts when it comes to prayer.

Jesus Gives Us His Own Authority

The first sign of a follower of Jesus is that he believes his Lord. We don't follow the Lord at all if we raise any questions about things that He speaks positively on. As far as true Christians are concerned, though a doctrine might be surrounded with ten thousand difficulties, the authority of the Lord Jesus sweeps them all away. Our Master's declaration is all the argument we want. *"And I tell you,"* is our logic. Reason! We see you at your best in Jesus, for God has made Him to be our wisdom. He cannot make a mistake. He cannot lie, and if He says, *"And I tell you,"* that is the end of all debate.

But there are certain reasons that should lead us even more confidently to trust in our Master's word on this point. There is power in every word of the Lord Jesus, but there is a special authority when those words are spoken.

There is an argument against the possibility of prayers being able to be answered, because the laws of nature are unalterable, and they must and will go on whether men pray or not. The claim is that not one drop of water will change its position in an ocean wave and not one particle of infectious disease can be stopped, even though all the Christians in the universe might plead against storms and epidemics. Concerning this matter, we are in no hurry to reply; those who object, have more to prove than we have, and among the rest, they have to prove a negative.

For us, it doesn't seem necessary to prove that the laws of nature are disturbed. God can work miracles, and He can still do them again the same way He did in days gone past. However, the Christian faith is not built on God having to do miracles in order to answer prayers. In order to fulfill a promise, a person has to rearrange everything and stop all the machinery of his day-to-day life in order to make it happen—it proves that we are just humans and that our wisdom and power are limited.

BUT HE IS GOD. Without reversing the engine or removing a single cog from a wheel, He fulfills the desires of His people as they come before Him. The Lord is so omnipotent that He can bring about a result, which we would call a miracle, without breaking any natural laws in the slightest degree. It's true that He did stop the machinery of the universe to answer prayer in biblical times, but today, with as much godlike glory as back then, He orders events so that believing prayers can be answered without disturbing the laws of nature. But this is not the only or main reason we can be secure and content. It's found in being able to hear the voice of someone who is competent to speak on the matter, and He says, "*I tell you, ask, and it will be given to you; seek, and you will find.*" It doesn't matter whether the laws of nature are reversible or irreversible, "*Ask and it will be given to you; seek, and you will find.*"

Now, who is it that speaks like this? It is He who made all things, without whom nothing that was made was made. Is He not able or entitled to speak about this? Oh, You eternal Word, You who were in the beginning with God, balancing the clouds, and setting the foundations of the earth, You know what the laws and the unchangeable components of nature may be, and if you say, "*Ask and it will be given to you,*" then it will be that way, regardless of the natural laws.

Added to that, we recognize God as the One who sustains all things, and since all the laws of nature can only operate because of His power and are maintained in motion by His might, He must be aware of all the forces in the world and how they work. If He says, *"Ask and it will be given to you,"* then He does not speak ignorantly but knows what He is stating. We can then be confident that there are no forces that can prevent the Lord's own word from being fulfilled. When the Creator and the Sustainer says the words, *"And I tell you,"* then that settles all controversy forever.

But there is another argument that has been around for some time and seems to be very solid and convincing. Rather than being raised by skeptics, it has come from those who hold a part of the truth. They state that prayer can produce nothing because God's commands and statutes have settled everything, and those decrees are irreversible. Now, we don't want to try and deny the claim that God's decrees have settled all events. We believe that God has already seen, knows, and predestined everything that happens in heaven above, or on the earth below. We agree that the foreknown position of a reed by the river is as predetermined as the position of a king, and "The husks of wheat from the hand of the winnower are steered the same as the stars in their paths."

Predestination embraces the great and the small and reaches all things. The question is, then why pray? Could we not also logically ask why bother breathing, eating, moving, or doing anything? We do have an answer that satisfies our questions, and that is, our prayers are in the predestination, and that God has ordained His people's prayers as much as anything else. And when we pray, we are producing links in the chain of ordained facts. Destiny commands that I should pray, so then I pray. Destiny commands that I will be answered, and the answer comes to me.

Even more than that, when it comes to other matters, we never order our actions by the unknown laws of God. For example, a person never questions whether they will eat or drink, because it might or might not be decreed that they will eat or drink; a person never asks whether they will work or not based on if it has been ordered how much or how little they will do. In the same way, it is inconsistent with common sense to make the secret orders of God a guide to us in our general day-to-day lives, so we feel it is with prayer, and so, we carry on and pray.

But there is still a better answer than all of these. Jesus comes forward, and He says to us this morning, "My dear children, do not let the decrees of God worry you. They are not inconsistent with your prayers being heard. *'I tell you, ask, and it will be given to you.'*" Now, who is He who says this? Why it is He who has been with the Father from the beginning (John 1:1), and He knows what the purposes of the Father are, and what the heart of God is, for He has told us in another place, *"The Father himself loves you"* (John 16:27).

Now, since He knows the orders of the Father and the heart of the Father, He can tell us, as an eyewitness, that there is nothing in the eternal purposes of God that conflicts with this truth: The person that asks, receives, and the person that seeks, finds. He has read the decrees from beginning to end. He has taken the Book and broken the seven seals on it open and declared the ordinances of heaven. He tells us that nothing in there is inconsistent with us bending our knees in prayer, and with the Father opening the windows of heaven to pour down the blessings that we are asking for.

On top of this, He is God. The purposes of heaven are His own purposes and having ordered those purposes, He assures us that there is nothing that will prevent the power and value of prayer. *"And I tell you."* If we just believe in Him, our doubts will be scattered in the wind, and we will know that He hears prayer.

But sometimes, a third difficulty in terms of prayer comes into our thoughts, linked to our own judgment of ourselves and our estimation of God. We feel that God is great and mighty, and we tremble in the presence of His Majesty. We feel that we are very small and sinful, and it does seem an incredible thing that such guilty nothings like ourselves should have power to move the hand that moves the world. I am sure that question often becomes an obstacle for us in prayer. But Jesus answers us so sweetly. He says, *"I tell you, ask, and it will be given to you."* Who is it that says, "I tell you"? Why, it is He who knows both the greatness of God and the weakness of man. He is God and out of His incredible Majesty, I can hear Him say, *"I tell you, ask, and it will be given to you."*

But Jesus was also a man, like ourselves, and He says, "Don't be afraid because you are small, for I, bone of your bone, and flesh of your flesh, assure you that God hears man's prayer." The words come to us with the harmony of blended notes.

The God, the man, both speak to us, "Don't be afraid of My Majesty, your prayer is heard. Don't be afraid of your own weakness. I, as a man, have been heard by God."

And if the shame and fear of sin haunt us and our own sorrow depresses us, I will remind you that Jesus, when He says, *"I tell you,"* gives us the authority of His person and His experience. Jesus was used to praying, and no one has ever prayed the way He did. He spent nights in prayer and whole days in sincere intercession and He says to us, *"I tell you, ask, and it will be given to you."*

I can picture Him coming straight from the grass of the hills, where He had knelt all night to pray, and He says, "My disciples, Ask, and it will be given to you, for I have prayed, and it has been given to Me." I can almost hear Him saying it with His face red like blood and His clothes soaked, as He rises from Gethsemane with His heart filled with sorrow, even to death. In that moment, when He was troubled, He was heard and so, He says to us, *"I tell you…knock, and it will be opened to you."*

Yes, and I think I can hear Him speak the same words from the cross, with His face lit up with the first rays of sunlight after He had taken our sins in His own body on the tree and had suffered all our griefs to the last agonizing pain. He had cried, *"My God, my God, why have you forsaken me"* (Matt 27:46), and when He received an answer, He cried in triumph, *"It is finished"* (John 19:30). In doing this, He invites us to also *"ask, and it will be given to you."* Jesus has proven the power of prayer.

"But" someone might say, "He didn't prove what it's like to pray in troubles like mine." How terrible to judge the Savior's trouble as worse than your own. There are no depths so deep that He has not dived to the bottom of them. Jesus prayed from the lowest dungeon and out of the most horrible pit. "Yes, but He didn't cry out because of the burden of sin." How can you speak so thoughtlessly! There has never been such a great burden of sin carried by any person as the one that was put on Him. True, the sins were not His own, but they were sins—sins with all their crushing weight in them. But was Jesus heard and was He helped in the end? Yes! In His own experience, Jesus gives us the proof that asking will be followed by receiving, even when sin lies at the door.

If as believers, we can't believe in the power and effectiveness of prayer based on Jesus' own words, then it will become very difficult and strange for us since our whole heart is leaning on Him. If He is not genuine and real, then you trust a false Savior. If He doesn't speak the truth, then we are deceived. If we can trust Him with our hearts, then there is no way we cannot trust Him with our prayers.

Also remember that if Jesus could speak so positively then, there is still a greater reason for believing in Him now, because He has gone in through the veil, and He sits at the right hand of God the Father. The voice we hear doesn't come to us from the Man of poverty, who is still wearing a seamless garment, but from the Priest on the throne with the golden belt around His waist. He is the One at the right hand of God who says, *"I tell you, ask, and it will be given to you."*

Do you believe in His name? If so, how can a prayer that is sincerely offered in that name fall uselessly to the ground and not reach heaven? When you bring your request in Jesus' name, a part of His authority covers your prayers so that if your prayer is rejected, you can't believe He is discredited. You have trusted Him, then believe that a prayer that is offered through Him must and will win the day.

Rather than spending more time talking on this point, we will trust the Holy Spirit to make it clear to all our hearts.

Jesus Presents Us with a Promise.

Notice that the promise is given to several types of prayer. *"I tell you, ask, and it will be given to you; seek, and you will find; knock, and it will be opened to you."* The verse clearly states that all forms of true prayer will be heard, as long as they are presented through Jesus Christ, and are for promised blessings. Some are vocal prayers, where people *ask*—we should never stop from continually and every day offering up the kind of prayer that comes from our mouths because the promise is that the one who asks will be heard.

But there are others who practice vocal prayer but are also more involved in active prayer. Through using humble and diligent ways, they *seek* the blessings that they need. Their heart speaks to God in its longings, strivings, emotions, and labors. Let them not stop seeking, for they will surely find. Then some combine the most passionate types, both acting and speaking because *knocking* is a loud kind of asking and a fervent form of seeking.

Whether our prayers are vocally talking to God or if they are more practical in their approach, or if they are a combination of both, or just expressed through a tear or a sigh, or even if they are expressed only in a trembling desire, they will be heard. All forms of true prayer will get responses from heaven.

Now have a look at how these varieties of prayer are put on an ascending scale. First, we are told to *ask*. I suppose that refers to the prayer, which is just stating what we want, telling the Lord that we would like this and that, and asking Him to give it to us. But as we learn the art of prayer, we go on further to *seek*, which shows that we order our arguments, and give reasons for our desires to be granted, and we begin to wrestle with God for the mercies needed. And if the blessings don't come, we then rise to the third degree, which is *knocking*, we become persistent. We are not content with asking and giving reasons, but we become more sincere and passionate in our requests. We begin to put into practice the verse that says, *"The kingdom of heaven has suffered violence, and the violent take it by force"* (Matt 11:12).

So, prayers grow from asking, which is the statement, to seeking, which is the pleading, to knocking, which is the persistence. For each of these stages of prayer, there is a distinct promise. The person that asks will have, what more did they ask for but what they got? But the one who seeks, going further in their prayer, shall find, enjoy, take hold of, and know that they have obtained. And those who knock will go even further than that for they will understand, and to them, the precious thing will be opened. They will not just have the blessing and enjoy it but will understand it. They will, *"comprehend with all the saints what is the breadth and length and height and depth"* (Eph 3:18).

However, I want you to notice this fact, which covers all—whatever form your prayer may take, it will succeed. If you only ask, you will receive. If you seek, you will find. If you knock it will be opened. But in each case, according to your faith, it will be for you. The clauses of the promise before us are not linked jointly as in legal terms—those that ask and seek, and knock shall receive. They are put separately—those that ask shall have, they that seek shall find, and whoever knocks shall have it opened. It is not when we combine the whole three that we get the blessing (although it's true that if we did combine them, we should get the combined reply), but if we practice only one of these three types of prayer, we will still get the thing that our hearts desire.

These three methods of prayer require different characteristics. An interpretation of our main verse says that faith asks, hope seeks, and love knocks, and it is an interpretation that is worth looking at. Faith asks because it believes that God will give. When hope asks, it expects, and therefore, seeks for the blessing. Love comes nearer and will not accept a refusal from God, but desires to enter into His house and to eat with Him, and so, will knock at His door until He opens.

But, let us remember what we have already seen: it doesn't matter which characteristic is exercised, a blessing will still be received. If faith asks, it will receive. If hope seeks, it will find, and if love knocks, it will be opened to her.

These three forms of prayer suit us in different stages of trouble. Imagine me, a poor beggar at mercy's door. I **ask**, and I shall receive, but then I lose my way and I can't find the One that I asked from. Well, then, I may *seek* with the confidence that I will find. And if I find myself in a worse position, not just poor and confused, but so sinful that I feel shut off from God like a leper banished out of the camp, then, I may *knock* and the door will open to me.

Each of these different descriptions of prayer is very simple. If anybody said, "I can't ask," we would reply, "You don't understand the word—everybody can ask." A child can ask. Long before a baby can speak, it can ask, it doesn't need to use words in order to ask for what it wants. No one is unable to ask. Prayers don't need to be eloquent.

I believe that God hates eloquent prayers. If a person asks you for help in elegant sentences, they will probably not get it. Fine clothes or language means nothing if someone is in desperate need of help. I heard a man begging loudly in the street one day using incredible speech. His language and style were grand and arrogant. I am sure he thought he would get lots of money because of his adopted way of talking. Instead of giving him anything, I just wanted to laugh at his nonsense.

Aren't most incredible prayers as useless as that man's begging? Many prayers in a meeting are far too eloquent and articulate. Keep your figures of speech, metaphors, and idiomatic expressions for your friends and family. Use them if you need to teach someone about something, but don't parade them before God. When we pray, the simpler our prayers are the better; the plainest, humblest language that expresses what we want to say is the best.

The next word is **seek**. Surely, there is no difficulty with seeking? It might be hard to *find*, but when it comes to seeking, there is no problem. When the woman in the parable lost her money, she lit a candle and looked for it. I don't suppose she had ever been to university or qualified as a doctor, or that she could have sat on the school board as a superior, but she could seek. Anybody who desires to do so can seek if it's a man, woman, or child. And to encourage them, the promise is not made in some kind of philosophical seeking, but quite simply, "The person that seeks finds."

Then, there is **knocking**. That is also something that is not very difficult. We used to do it when we were boys, often irritating our neighbors. If the door-knocker on the door was a bit too high, we had other ways and means of knocking at the door: a stone would do it, or the heel of a shoe, *anything* could make a knocking sound. It was not something that was too hard to do. Therefore, Jesus makes the statement in these words to tell us, "You don't need an education, training, or talent, and no intellect for prayer; ask, seek, knock, that is all. The promise applies to each of these ways of praying.

Will you believe the promise? It is Jesus who gives it. No lie came from His lips. Don't doubt Him. Carry on praying if you have already prayed, but if you have never prayed before, God help you to begin today!

Jesus Testifies that Prayer Is Heard

Having given us a promise, Jesus then adds, "You can be very sure that this promise will be fulfilled, not only because I say it, but because it is and always has been that way." When a man says the sun will rise tomorrow morning, we believe it because it has always risen. Jesus tells us, as an indisputable fact throughout the ages, that true asking has been followed by receiving. Remember that He who stated this fact knew it. If you state a fact, someone might say, "Yes, as far as your observation goes, it is true." But the observation of Christ is limitless.

No true prayer has ever been offered to Him that He was not aware of. Prayers acceptable with God go up by the way of the wounds of Christ. So, Jesus can speak from personal knowledge and His declaration is that prayer has succeeded —"Everyone that asks, receives, and those that seek, find."

Now, we must look at the limitations that can be made by our own ordinary common sense and those found in the Bible. Everyone who carelessly or wrongly asks or pretends to ask of God doesn't get what they ask for. God will not answer every silly, trivial, thoughtless request of people who have not been born again. When we look at the verse, common sense makes it clear of this limit.

The Bible puts its own restriction on it by saying, *"You ask and do not receive, because you ask wrongly"* (James 4:3). If you don't ask correctly, you will never receive. If we ask so that we can eat and use the things that we lust for, we will not get them. If we ask for things that would not be good for us, then our prayers will be heard but the answer will not be what we are hoping for. With this in mind, what Jesus says has no other restrictions, "Everyone that asks receives."

However, we must also remember that often, when the ungodly and the wicked have asked God for something, they have received. In their time of trouble, they have called on God and He has answered them. "How can you say that?" someone asks. I don't say it, the Bible does. Ahab's prayer was answered and the Lord said, *"Have you seen how Ahab has humbled himself before me? Because he has humbled himself before me, I will not bring the disaster in his days; but in his son's days I will bring the disaster upon his house"* (1 Kings 21:29).

The Lord also heard the prayer of Jehoahaz, the son of Jehu, who did evil in the sight of the Lord (2 Kings 13:1-4). The Israelites too, because of their sins they were handed over to their enemies, and they cried to God for deliverance and were answered. But God Himself even said that they only flattered Him with their words. Does this surprise you? Does He not hear the young birds when they cry? Do you think He will not hear people that have been formed in His own image? Do you doubt it?

Remember Nineveh. The prayers offered at Nineveh, were they spiritual prayers? Have you ever heard of a church in Nineveh? I haven't, nor do I believe that the Ninevites were ever converted. But, because of Jonah's preaching, they were convinced that they were in danger from the great Jehovah, and they fasted and humbled themselves. God heard their prayer and for a while, Nineveh was preserved.

Many times, in their sickness and hardship, God has heard the prayers of the ungrateful and the evil. Do you think God only gives to those who are good? Have you lived at the foot of Mount Sinai and learned to judge according to the law of merit? What were you when you began to pray? Were you good and righteous? Hasn't God commanded you to do good to those who are evil? Will He command you to do what He won't do? Hasn't He said that He *"sends rain on the just and on the unjust"* (Matt 5:45), and does that not happen? Isn't He daily blessing those who curse Him and doing good to those who spitefully use Him? This is one of the glories of God's grace. When there is nothing else good in a person, but a cry is lifted from their heart, the Lord often bends down to send relief from trouble.

Now, if God has even heard the prayers of people who have not looked for Him in a holy and righteous manner and has temporarily delivered them in answer to their cries, will He not hear you when you humble yourself before Him and desire to be reconciled to Him? Surely the reasoning is clear to see.

But if we look closer at real, spiritual prayers, then it is clear that everyone that asks receives without any limit. There has never been a case of a person who is really seeking spiritual blessings from God and has not received them. The tax collector stood far off and his heart was so broken that he dared not look up to heaven, yet God looked down on him.

Manasseh lay in a deep dungeon. He had been a cruel persecutor of the people of God. There was nothing in him that could commend him to God, but God still heard him in the dungeon and brought freedom to his soul. Through his own sin, Jonah found himself in the belly of a whale. He was an angry, disobedient servant of God, but out of the fish's stomach he cried, and God heard him. *"everyone who asks receives, and the one who seeks finds, and to the one who knocks it will be opened."* **Everyone.**

If I wanted evidence, I could find it in any church. I could ask those that are born again to testify that God has heard their prayers. I don't believe that there is one person who has gone to hell that can say, "I sought the Lord and He rejected me." On Judgment Day, you will not find one single person that can say, "I knocked at mercy's door, but God refused to open it." No one who will one day stand before the great white throne can plead, "Oh Jesus, I would have been saved by You, but You would not save me. I gave myself up into Your hands, but You rejected me. I repented and asked for mercy from You, but I did not receive it."

Everyone that asks receives. It has been that way right up to this day, it will be so until Jesus comes back. If you doubt it, try it, and if you have tried it, try it again. Are you in ragged clothes? That doesn't matter, *everyone* that asks receives. Are you filled with sin? That makes no difference, *everyone* who seeks finds. Do you feel as if you were completely shut out from God? That doesn't matter either, "Knock, and it *will* be opened to you, for everyone that asks receives." "Is there no election there?" I am very sure there is, but that does not change this truth that has no limit to it whatsoever—*"everyone."* What a rich verse it is. *"Everyone* that asks receives."

When our Lord spoke these words, He could have pointed to His own life as evidence. We can refer to it now and show that no one that asked Jesus for something did not receive it. The Syro-Phoenician woman was at first offended when the Lord called her a dog, but when she had the courage to say, *"Yet even the dogs eat the crumbs that fall from their masters' table"* (Matt 15:27), she soon discovered that everyone that asks receives. The woman who came up behind Him in the crowd and touched the hem of His garment, she was no asker, but she was a seeker and she found.

I am sure in answer to all that's been said, someone will cry and say, "I have been calling out to God for a long time for salvation. I have asked, I have sought, and I have knocked, but it has not come yet." Well, dear friend, if I had to say who is true between God or you, I know which I will choose, and I would advise you to believe God before you believe yourself. God will hear prayer, but do you know there is one thing before prayer? What is it? The Gospel does not say, "He who prays will be saved." That is not the Gospel. I believe he will be saved, but that is not the Gospel. I am told to preach to you. *"Go into all the world and proclaim the gospel to the whole creation. Whoever believes and is baptized will be saved"* (Mark 16:15-16).

Now, you have been asking God to save you, do you expect Him to save you without you believing and being baptized? Hopefully, you have not had the audacity to ask God to ignore His own Word! He may say to you, "Do as I command you, believe My Son. He that believes in Him has everlasting life." Let me ask you, do you believe in Jesus Christ? Will you trust Him? "Oh, I trust Him," you may say, "I trust Him completely." Don't ask for salvation anymore, you have it already, you are saved. If you trust Jesus with all your heart, your sins are forgiven, and you are saved.

And the next time you approach the Lord, go with praise as well as with prayer, and sing and bless His name. "But how do I know that I am saved?" you might ask. God says, *"Whoever believes and is baptized will be saved."* Have you believed? Have you been baptized? If so, you are saved. How do I know that? Based on the best evidence in all the world—God says you are. Do you need any more evidence than that?

"I want to feel it." Feel! Are your feelings better than God's confirmation? Will you make God a liar by asking for more signs and evidence than the word of His testimony? I have no other evidence that I should trust in concerning my salvation except for this, that I rest only in Christ with all my heart, soul, and strength. "Other refuge have I none," and if you have that evidence, it's all the proof that you need to seek for today. Other evidence of the grace in your heart shall come in time, gather around you, and reinforce the doctrines you hold on to, but your first business now is to believe in Jesus.

"I have asked for faith," you might say. Well, what do you mean by that? To believe in Jesus Christ is the gift of God, but it must be your own action as well. Do you think God will believe for you or that the Holy Ghost believes instead of us? What must the Holy Spirit believe? You must believe for yourself or be lost. He cannot lie. Will you believe in Him or not? He deserves to be believed. Trust in Him and you are saved, and your prayer is answered.

Another person might even say, "I trust I am already saved, but I have been looking for the salvation of others in answer to my prayers." Dear friend, you will get it. *"Everyone who asks receives, and the one who seeks finds, and to the one who knocks it will be opened."* "But I have sought for this other person's conversion with many prayers for years." You will have it, or you will one day be shown why you don't have it, and you will be content in that. Pray on in hope. Many people have died before their prayers for others were answered.

There is the story of a father who had prayed for many years for his sons and daughters, and yet they were not born again, instead, they all became very worldly. The time came when he was about to die. He gathered his children around his bed, hoping to testify and be a witness for Jesus that this might bring about their conversion. But unfortunately, he was deeply troubled in his own heart. He had doubts about his own salvation and love for the Lord. He was one of God's children who died in the dark. For him, this was his worst fear, that his dear children would see his despair, and be turned against wanting any kind of religion.

The good man was buried and his sons came to the funeral. God heard the man's prayer that day, because as they left the grave, one of them said to the other, "Brother, our father died very unhappy." "He did, brother. I was so surprised by it because I never knew a better man than our father." "Ah," said the first brother, "if a holy man such as our father found dying such a hard thing, it would be terrible for us who have no faith when our time comes."

They all had the same thoughts, and it brought them to the cross. So, the good man's prayer was heard in a mysterious way. Heaven and earth shall pass away, but while God lives, prayer must be heard. While God remains true to His Word, supplication is not in vain. May the Lord give you grace to continually practice it. Amen.

(A sermon on January 19, 1873, at the Metropolitan Tabernacle, Newington)

Study Guide

Successful prayer is something we all long for and wish we knew how to achieve. Spurgeon does an amazing job of breaking it down into easy-to-understand components. This study guide is not meant to add or subtract from anything already said, but to help in concentrating your mind more onto the topic already discussed. There is no formula or format to working through them, but should rather be seen as stimulants for discussion and thought.

1. What is your view on miracles? Have you ever seen or witnessed one?
2. The phrase, "I tell you" is used as proof that if God has said something, then it is good enough for us to simply believe it. How much do you take God's words and promises at 'face-value' and trust Him to do what He has said?
3. Spurgeon categorizes prayer into 3 different types: Ask, seek, and knock. Which one do you fall into?

4. Read James 4:1-10. Now, look back at the reason we often do not receive in verse 3. What do you understand by this passage when read as a whole?
5. Reading Matthew 5:45, we could say that if God will bless the unrighteous as well as Christians, why should we bother praying. What do you think? Compare this with Proverbs 15:29.
6. As humans, we want to feel something as confirmation that it is real or has happened. Spurgeon talks about our feelings when it comes to prayer, do you agree with what he says?
7. If you had to rate your own prayer life right now out of 10 (1 being worst, and 10 being excellent), what would your score be? Why?

2

THE RAVEN'S CRY

"He gives to the beast their food, and to the young ravens that cry."
Psalm 147:9

We will open with a quote from Joseph Caryl on ravens. "Naturalists tell us that when the raven has fed his young in the nest until they are fully-fledged and able to fly abroad, he pushes them out of the nest, and will not let them stay there, but puts them out to get their own living. Now when these young ones are on their first flight from their nest and are hardly acquainted with ways to help themselves with food, then the Lord provides it for them. It is said by credible authorities that the raven is marvelously strict and severe in this, for as soon as his young ones are able to provide for themselves, he will not fetch any more food for them. Yes, some agree that the old ones will not allow them to even stay in the same country where they were bred, and if so, then they must wander. Proverbially we say, 'Need makes the old wife walk.' We could also say, 'and the young ones too.'"

Some parents force their children out of the home as soon as they can look after themselves and are able and competent to get their own food, the same way the raven does to his young ones out of the nest. Now, in the verse when the babies of the raven are in this predicament, and are thrown out, and can't find their own food yet, who does it say will provide for them? Isn't it the Lord? Just as He provided for the old raven, won't He also provide for his young ones, while they live in the nest and when they are evicted without any food?

Solomon sent the lazy man to go and watch the ant, and to learn lessons from rock rabbits, greyhounds, and spiders. Let us be open to being taught by any of God's creatures, and look at the ravens' nest to learn as though we are in a school.

To the pure, there is nothing unclean, and to the wise, there is nothing trivial. Let's put aside any superstitious fear of the raven as an omen of bad luck so that all we see is a glossy, black-winged bird. Let's be willing to see more than that, and we will be rewarded if we are teachable. Noah's raven didn't bring him back an olive branch, but ours might as we look at it. The ravens might even bring us meat just as they did when Elijah was fed by them at Cherith's stream.

Jesus once gave a very powerful assertion from ravens—an argument that was intended to comfort and encourage those of His servants who were filled with needless worries about their temporary circumstances. To these disciples he said, *"Consider the ravens: they neither sow nor reap, they have neither storehouse nor barn, and yet God feeds them. Of how much more value are you than the birds!"* (Luke 12:24). Following His logic—which you will agree was solid, because He always told the truth—I will continue in the same line of argument.

Consider the ravens as they cry; with their harsh, inarticulate, croaking notes they make their needs known, and your heavenly Father answers their prayer and sends them food. You have also begun to pray and to seek His favor, are you not much better than them? Does God care for the ravens, and won't He also care for you? Does He hear the cries of the unfledged ravens in their nests, when they are hungry and cry to Him and wait to be fed?

Does He supply them in answer to their cries, and won't He also answer you, poor trembling people that are seeking His face and favor through Jesus? This will be my aim here: simply to work that one thought out. My aim, with the Holy Spirit, is to say something to those who have been praying for mercy, but still have not received it. Who has gone on their knees, perhaps for months, with one very bitter cry, but still don't have any peace.

Their sin still hangs like a millstone about their neck. They sit in the valley of the shadow of death. No light has shone on them, and they are rubbing their hands and moaning, "Has God forgotten to be gracious? Has He closed His ear to the prayers of seeking hearts? Won't He listen to sinners' pitiful cries anymore? Will the tears of those who repent not move Him to have compassion?" Satan is also telling those of you who are now in this state of mind, that God will never hear you, that He will let you cry until you die, that you will gasp out your life in sighs and tears, and that you will be thrown into the lake of fire at the end.

I hope to give you some comfort and encouragement. I want to motivate you to cry out more passionately. Come to the cross and take hold of it, and promise that you will never leave it until you find the gift that you are seeking. I want to stir you, with the Holy Spirit's help, so that you can say as Queen Esther did, *"I will go to the king...and if I perish, I perish"* (Esther 4:16). And may you also add to that the vow of Jacob, *"I will not let you go unless you bless me!"* (Gen 32:26).

This is the question we are asking: **God hears the young ravens, won't He also hear you?** I argue that He does for many reasons.

You Are Worth More than a Raven

The raven is nothing more than a poor, unclean bird, whose instant death would not be a great loss to creation. If thousands of ravens were killed tomorrow, I don't think that there would be any overwhelming grief and sorrow over it. It would simply be a number of poor dead birds, and that would be all. But you are an immortal soul. The raven is gone when life is over, there is no more raven, but when your life on earth is finished, you have not ceased to exist. You have been launched out onto the sea of life, you have just started to live forever.

You will see earth's massive mountains crumble to nothing before your immortal spirit expires. The moon's feeble light will fade, and the sun's mighty fires will be extinguished in complete darkness, and yet your spirit will still carry on in its everlasting journey— an everlasting journey of misery unless God hears your cry.

"Oh, that truth immense,

This mortal, immortality shall wear!

The pulse of mind can never cease to play;

By God awakened, it forever throbs,

Eternal as His own eternity!

Above the angels, or below the fiends:

To mount in glory, or in shame descend—

Mankind is destined by resistless doom."

—Robert Montgomery.

Do you think that God will hear the poor bird that is here one moment and gone the next, but will not hear an immortal soul like you, whose life will carry on just as His own? It must make you think that if He hears the dying raven, He will also hear an undying person. It was said by those in ancient Greece, that the mythical god, Jupiter, had no time to worry about little things, but Jehovah bends down to care for the least of His creatures and even looks into nests. Will He not care mercifully for spirits who are heirs of eternity?

I also never heard of ravens being made in the image of God, but I do know that even though our human race is defiled, deformed, and debased, God originally said, *"Let us make man in our image"* (Gen 1:26). There is something about man which cannot be found in the lower creatures, the best and worthiest of whom are ranked far below the worst descendant of Adam. Looking at the creation of man, his mind, and even in the adaptation of his body to assist the mind, there is a wonderful display of the wisdom of the Most High. Find the most deformed, obscure, and wicked of our race, and rather than flatter the nature of humans, there is still a dignity about people that can't be found in any of the animals on earth.

The biblical beasts, Behemoth and Leviathan, are in subjection to man. The eagle can't soar as high as a man's soul can, nor can the lion feed on such royal meat as man's spirit hungers after. And do you still think that God will hear such a low, mean creature like the raven, and yet not hear you, when you are part of the race that was formed in His own image? Oh! Don't think so harshly and foolishly of the One whose ways are always fair and just!

I will ask this question: Doesn't nature teach that man is to be cared for above the birds of the air? If you heard the cries of young ravens, you might feel enough compassion to give them food, if you knew how to feed them. But I can't believe that any of you would help the birds, and not have the compassion to fly to the rescue of a dying baby who you might hear crying because it was left by cruel neglect. If you heard the sad cry of a sick man passing away in the quiet night, left out in the streets, wouldn't you get up and help him? If you'd help a raven, then I'm sure you would. If you have any compassion for a raven, surely you would have much more pity for a man.

I know there are examples of some simple-minded people who care more for homeless dogs than for homeless men and women, and yet it's far more likely that those who feel something for dogs are those who care most lovingly for other people. Regardless, if I was in need of any help, I'm sure I would find it in them. And don't you think that God, the All-Wise One, when He cares for these unfledged birds in the nest, will also be sure to care for you? Your heart says, "Yes." Then begin answering any doubt in your heart by turning its own logical reasoning against it.

But I hear you say, "The raven is not as sinful as I am. It may be an unclean bird, but it can't be as morally unclean as I am. It may be black in color, but I am black with sin. A raven can't break the Sabbath, can't swear, can't commit adultery. A raven can't be a drunk, it can't defile itself with bad habits like those that are polluting me." I know all that, and it might seem that your case is hopeless, but I don't think it really does.

Just think of it for a minute. What does this prove? That you are a creature capable of sinning, and consequently, that you are an intelligent spirit living in a sense in which a raven does not live. You are a spiritual creature moving in the spirit world. You belong to the world of souls in which the raven has no part. The raven can't sin, because it has no spirit, no soul, but you are an intelligent being, and the best part of you is your soul.

Now, the soul is far more precious than the body, and the raven (as we understand) is nothing but the body. You, however, are evidently soul as well as body, or else you would not be capable of sinning. Here, I can see a glimmer of light in that black, discouraging thought. Does God care for flesh, blood, bones, and black feathers? Won't He also care for your reason, will, judgment, conscience, and immortal soul?

If you just think about it, you will see that a raven's cry can't be heard by the ear of divine benevolence, and yet for your prayer to be despised and disregarded by the Most High.

"The insect that with puny wing,

Just shoots along one summer's ray;

The flower which the breath of Spring

Wakes into life for half a day;

The smallest grain, the most softest hair,

All feel our heavenly Father's care."

Surely then He will respect the cry of the humble, and will not refuse their prayer.

Before leaving this point, let's look at the mention of a raven that should encourage a sinner. As an author once wrote, "Among birds, He does not mention the hawk or falcon, which are highly prized and fed by princes, nor the sweet singing nightingale, or musical pretty birds that men keep and delight in, but He chooses that hateful and malicious bird, the croaking raven, whom no one values except to eat up the carrion which might annoy him."

See then, and wonder at the wisdom and kindness of God, that He should provide food for the raven, a creature of such a dark color, and such a harsh tone, that is so disgusting to most men and ominous to some. There is a great providence of God seen in providing for the ant, who gathers her food in summer, but more so for the raven, who forgets or is careless to provide for himself, yet God provides for him."

One would think God should say to the ravens that they must take care of themselves or die. No, the Lord doesn't despise anything He has created. The raven is made by God, and therefore will be provided for by Him. Not only the fair, innocent dove, but the ugly raven has his food from God. This clearly shows that the lack of excellence in you—you black, raven-like sinner—will not stop your cry from being heard in heaven. The blood of Jesus will remove any unworthiness, and He will completely clean away your corruption. Just believe in Jesus and you will find peace.

Your Cry Is Different to the Raven's

When the young ravens cry, I suppose they don't really know what they want. They have a natural instinct that makes them cry for food, but their cry doesn't actually express what they want. You can easily work out that they mean food, but they have no articulate speech. They don't say a single word. It's just a constant, croaking, craving cry, and that's all.

But you do know what you want, and even though your words are few, your heart knows its own bitterness and awful troubles. Your sighs and groans have an obvious meaning. Your understanding and the needs of your heart are closely linked. You know that you want peace and forgiveness. You know that you need Jesus—His precious blood, His perfect righteousness. Now, if God hears such a strange, chattering, indistinct cry like the raven's, don't you think that He will also hear the rational and expressive prayer of a poor, needy, guilty soul who is crying out to Him, "God be merciful to me, a sinner"? Surely, your logic tells you that!

There is also a difference in that ravens cannot use arguments, for they have no understanding. They can't say,

"He knows what arguments I'd take

To wrestle with my God,

I'd plead for His own mercy's sake,

And for a Savior's blood."

They have only one argument, which is their main need that forces them to cry, but they can't go beyond this, set it in order, or describe it in a language. But you have a multitude of arguments you can give and you have an understanding to set them in order and use them to reach the throne of grace. If the insignificant request of the unspoken need of the raven can find God, how much more will you succeed with the Most High, if you can argue your case before Him, and come to Him with spoken arguments.

If you are in despair, come and try the Lord! I beg you, let that sad song ascend to the ears of mercy! Open your bursting heart and let it out in tears, if you can't find the words.

Sometimes, a raven has a great advantage over some sinners who seek God in prayer, because they are more sincere and passionate about their food than some of us are about our hearts. However don't let this discourage you, but see it as a reason why you should be more eager and devoted than you have been. When ravens want food, they don't stop crying until they have got it. You can't keep a hungry young raven quiet until his mouth is full, and there is no keeping a sinner quiet when he is really sincere until his heart is filled with divine mercy.

I wish that some of you prayed stronger and more passionately! *"The kingdom of heaven has suffered violence, and the violent take it by force"* (Matt 11:12). An old Puritan said, "Prayer is a cannon that is set at the gate of heaven to burst it open." You must take the city by storm if you want to receive it. You will not ride to heaven on a featherbed, you must go on a journey. There is no going to the land of glory while you are sound asleep; dreamy, lazy people will wake up in hell. If God has caused you to feel the need of salvation in your heart, cry like someone who is awake and alive. Be sincere. Cry aloud. Don't hold back. And then you will see that my argument makes sense: a reasonable, argumentative, intelligent prayer is more likely to succeed with God than the small, screaming, chattering noise of the raven, and if He hears the cry of a raven, there is no doubt that He will hear yours.

Your Prayer Is More Pleasant to God than a Raven's Cry

All that the young ravens call for is food. Give them a little meat and they are content. Your cry must be much more pleasing to God's ear because you ask for forgiveness through the blood of His dear Son. It is more worthy for the Most High to be giving spiritual than natural gifts. The streams of grace flow from the upper springs. I know He is so accommodating that He doesn't dishonor Himself even when He puts food into the young raven's mouth, but still, there is more honor in giving peace, pardon, and reconciliation to men and women.

Eternal love made a way of mercy before the foundation of the world was created, and infinite wisdom is engaged with limitless power to carry out the divine design. Surely the Lord must take great pleasure in saving men and women. If God is pleased to supply food for the animals, don't you think that He finds more delight in supplying His own children? I think it would be more satisfying for you to teach your own children, than simply feeding your animals, or scattering seeds for the birds, because it is something much greater and nobler, that requires all your effort and ability, and brings out your true self.

This is not a speculation or a guess, it's written in the Bible, *"He delights in steadfast love,"* or in some translations—mercy (Micah 7:18). When God uses His power He cannot be sad, for He is a happy God. But if it's possible for the Almighty God to be happier at one time than another, it's when He is forgiving sinners through the precious blood of Jesus.

As a sinner, when you cry to God you give Him an opportunity to do what He loves doing the most, because He delights to forgive, to take His Ephraim in his arms, to say of His prodigal son, *"For this my son was dead, and is alive again; he was lost, and is found"* (Luke 15:24). This is more satisfying to the Father's heart than the feeding of the 'fatted calf,' or looking after the cattle on a thousand hills.

You are asking for something which will be far more of an honor for God to give than the simple gift of food to ravens. This is my argumentative hammer bringing a very strong blow to break your doubt into pieces. May the Holy Spirit, the true Comforter, work in you mightily! Surely the God who gives food to ravens will not deny peace and forgiveness to sinners that are seeking it. Try Him! Try Him right now! Don't wait! Try Him now.

We Are Commanded to Cry to Him, Not the Ravens

We can't spend too much time on only one point when there is so much more to say on the whole subject. Another encouragement for us is that the ravens are not commanded to cry. When they do cry, they have not been given any special privilege By God, but you have a right to approach the throne of God in prayer, because of His own call to do so.

If a rich man opens his house to people who were not invited, then he would also have people coming in who were invited. Ravens come without being told to come, yet they are not sent away empty. You have been called and invited as a guest, how can you be denied entry? Do you think you are not called to come? Look at this:

- *"Everyone who calls on the name of the Lord will be saved"* (Rom 10:13).
- *"Call upon me in the day of trouble; I will deliver you, and you shall glorify me"* (Psalm 50:15).
- *"Go into all the world and proclaim the gospel to the whole creation. Whoever believes and is baptized will be saved, but*

whoever does not believe will be condemned" (Mark 16:15-16).
- *"Believe in the Lord Jesus, and you will be saved"* (Acts 16:31).
- *"Repent and be baptized every one of you in the name of Jesus Christ"* (Acts 2:38).

These are commands that are given to everyone, regardless of who they are. They freely invite you. No, they instruct you to come. After seeing this, how can you think that God will refuse you? The window is open, the raven flies in, and the God of mercy doesn't chase it out. The door is open, and the word of promise commands you to come—don't think that He will reject you, but rather believe that He will receive you with grace, love you freely, and then you will give him the *"vows of our lips"* (Hosea 4:2-4). But whatever you think about it, try Him! Try Him now!

The Raven's Cry Is Not a Work of Grace

This is another point that really enforces the argument. The cry of a young raven is nothing but the natural cry of a creature, but your cry, if it's sincere, is the result of a work of grace in your heart.

When the raven cries to heaven it's only the raven crying out, but when you say, "God be merciful to me, a sinner," it's really the Holy Spirit crying in you. It's the new life that God has given you crying to the source from which it came to have a deeper relationship and communication with Him. It needs God to establish a person who is praying in sincerity and in truth.

We can teach our children to 'say their prayers,' but we cannot teach them to 'pray.' You could make a 'prayer-book,' but you can't put any 'prayer' into a book, for it is something too spiritual to be restricted between pages. Some of you might 'read prayers' as a family. I will not condemn that, but I will say that you could read those 'prayers' for seventy years, but never actually pray, for prayer is quite a different thing than just words. True prayer is the exchange of your heart with God, and the heart never comes into spiritual commerce with the ports of heaven until the Holy Spirit puts wind into the sails and speeds the ship into its harbor. You must be born again. If there is any real prayer in your heart, though you may not know the secret, the Holy Spirit is there.

Now if He hears other cries that do not come from Himself, how much more will He hear those that do! Maybe you have wondered whether your cry is a natural or a spiritual one. This may seem very important, and it is, but whether your cry is one or the other, continue to seek the Lord. Maybe you doubt whether natural cries are heard by God. Let me assure you that they are.

I remember being in an Ultra-Calvinistic church preaching to some children about this, and encouraging them to pray. I said that long before I was born again, I had prayed for common things, and that God had heard my prayers. This did not sit well with those in charge, and afterward, they came to me asking what I had meant. but really to complain and grumble as they do. *"They surrounded me like bees!"* (Psalm

118:12). After some time, they resorted to calling me names. They began to ask what kind of Arminianism this was that I was preaching, and they found it amusing to give me the title of "Fullerism." I actually was honored and could have thanked them for it. But to say that God should hear the prayer of a non-Christian was something worse than Arminianism to them.

They then argued by quoting a verse, *'The [prayer] of the wicked is an abomination to the Lord.'* I very quickly answered by asking them to find that verse in the Bible, because I wanted to prove to them that the devil was the author of that saying and that it was not in the Bible at all. *"The sacrifice of the wicked is an abomination to the Lord"* (Prov 15:8) is in the Bible, and it means something very different from their version of the 'prayer of the wicked.'

Also, there is a significant difference between who was being referred to as 'wicked' in this instance, and the natural man that we are talking about now. I don't think a person who begins to pray in any form can be thought of as 'wicked' in the way Solomon intended when he wrote this. They are also definitely not the same as those that turn away from hearing the law and whose prayer is an abomination to God.

"But," they said to me, "how can God hear a natural, unspiritual prayer?" As I paused for a moment, an old woman in a red cloak pushed her way into the little circle that had gathered around me, and said to them very strongly, as though she were a mother in Israel, "Why do you ask this question, and forget what God has said! What are you saying, that God does not hear natural prayer?

Doesn't He hear the young ravens when they cry to Him and do you think they offer spiritual prayers?" Immediately, the men all left. It was a thorough defeat, and for once in their lives, they must have felt that it was possible for them to be mistaken.

This should be an encouragement and a comfort for us.

I'm not going to ask you to test whether your prayers are natural or spiritual, or if they come from God's Spirit or not, because that might discourage you. If the prayer comes from your heart, we know how it got there, even if you don't. God hears the ravens, and I do believe He will hear you. I also believe that He hears your prayer, because there is a secret work of the Holy Spirit going on inside of you, teaching you to pray, even if you are not aware of it.

You Don't Cry Alone like the Ravens

This is another very strong point in our argument—When the young ravens cry, they cry alone, but when you pray, you have One that is greater, praying with you.

When a sinner cries, "God be merciful to me, a sinner," can you hear another cry that goes up with his? No, you don't hear it, because your ears are deaf and not spiritually tuned, but God hears it. There is another voice, much louder and sweeter, and far more established, going up at the same time as the sinner, pleading, "Father, forgive them through my precious blood." The echo to the sinner's whisper is as majestic as the thunder's peal. No sinner can truly pray without Jesus praying at the same time. You can't see or hear

Him, but Jesus never stirs the depths of your heart by His Spirit without His soul being stirred, too.

When the prayer of a sinner comes before God, it's a very different thing from the one that first came out of his mouth. Sometimes poor people ask others to help them by taking their request to a large company or a more influential person. They bring their petition and ask us to present it as an intermediary. It's badly spelled, not well written, and we can hardly make out what they are trying to say, but there's enough for us to know what they want.

First, we write it out neatly for them, stating their case in the proper language. Then, we put our own name at the bottom. If we have any influence of our own, then that person will get what they want through the power of the name we have signed at the bottom of the petition. This is just what Jesus does with our poor prayers. He makes sense of them, stamps them with the seal of His own atoning blood, puts His own name at the bottom, and then they go up to God's throne. It's still our prayer, but it's His prayer, too. And because it's His prayer, then it will succeed.

Now, this is a hard-hitting, sledgehammer argument! If the ravens succeed when they cry all alone, and their poor chattering gets them what they want because of their own efforts, how much more will the poor, trembling sinner's pathetic requests succeed when they say, "For Jesus' sake." They can seal all their own arguments with the cry, "Jesus deserves it. Oh Lord, give it to me for His sake."

I trust that those who have been seeking and crying out for so long but are afraid that they will never be heard, will not have to wait much longer. I hope that soon they will have a gracious answer of peace, and if they don't receive the desire of their hearts now, that they may be encouraged to persevere until the day of grace dawns on them. You have a promise which the ravens don't have, another point in my argument we could discuss. With a promise attached to your request, don't worry —you will quickly enter the throne of grace!

I want to encourage anyone that is a sinner, **if you have cried out unsuccessfully, carry on crying out.** *"'Go again,' seven times"* (1 Kings 18:43), yes, even seventy times seven. Remember that the mercy of God in Jesus is your only hope. Hold onto it then as a drowning man grabs onto the only rope in his reach. If you die while still praying for mercy through the precious blood, you will be the first that ever died that way. Carry on crying out. Just carry on crying, but also believe, for believing brings the morning star and the dawn of a new day.

When John Ryland's wife, Betty, lay dying, she was very anxious and stressed, even though she had been a Christian for many years.

Her husband said to her in his strange, but wise way, "Well, Betty, what is worrying you?"

"Oh, John, I am dying and I have no hope!"

"But my dear, where are you going then?"

"I am going to hell!" was the answer.

"Well," he said, covering up his deep anguish with his usual humor, and meaning to strike a blow that would be sure to hit the nail on the head and chase away her doubts, "What are you going to do when you get there, Betty?" His wife could not answer, and Mr. Ryland continued, "Do you think you will pray when you get there?"

"Oh, John," she said, "I would pray anywhere. I can't help praying."

"Well then," he said, "they will say, 'Here is Betty Ryland praying in hell. Throw her out. We won't have anybody praying here. Throw her out.'"

This strange way of putting it brought light to her heart, and she saw at once how crazy it was to think that someone that was really seeking Jesus could be thrown out of His presence forever.

Carry on crying out. Carry on crying! While the child can cry, it lives. While you can still call on the throne of mercy, there is hope for you. But you must also hear as well as cry, and believe what you hear, for it's by believing that you will find peace.

But wait, there's more to say on this topic. Is it possible that you could already have received what you are crying for? You might say, "I wouldn't ask for something that I have already been given. If I knew I had it, I would stop asking, and begin praising and blessing God."

Now, I don't know what state you are in, but I am sure that there are some people who have already received the mercy that they are asking for. Instead of saying to them, "Seek my face," the Lord is saying, "Why are you crying out to me? I have heard you in your time of need, and I have given you what you asked for. I have blotted out your sins like a cloud, and your iniquities like a thick cloud. I have saved you. You are mine. I have cleansed you from all your sins. Rejoice." In this type of scenario, believing praise is more suitable than agonizing prayer.

Then you might also say, "But it's not possible for me to have received mercy while I am still seeking it." Well, I don't know. Sometimes mercy is like a woman that faints outside the gate of a house. She could be carried inside while not properly conscious, and yet she still thinks that she is outside by the gate. She can hear the dog barking, but when she comes around, she finds that she is safe inside. Some of you may have faded into discouragement just when you are coming to Jesus. May grace restore you.

What is it you're looking for? Some of you are expecting to see bright visions, but I hope you never get these because they are not worth it. All the visions in the world since the days of miracles are just dreams—dreams are nothing but vanity. People eat too much supper and then dream. It's indigestion or a very active brain, and that's it. If that's all the evidence you have of your conversion, then you should question if it's real. I pray that you don't become satisfied with it and build your eternal hopes on such nonsense.

Perhaps you are looking for very strange feelings—not an electric shock, but something very extraordinary and unusual. Believe me, you don't ever need to feel these emotions which you think so much of. All those strange feelings that some people speak of in connection with being born again are probably not worth much. I am sure that they are not necessary for salvation and have nothing to do with conversion.

Here are a few questions to think about.

Do you believe you are a sinner? "Yes," you answer. But supposing I take away that word "sinner"? Do you mean that you believe you have broken God's law, that you are a good-for-nothing offender against God's order? Do you believe that in your heart you have broken all the commandments and that you deserve punishment? "Yes," you answer, "I don't just believe that, but I feel it. It's a burden that I carry about with me every day."

Now, do you believe that Jesus can take all this sin of yours away? Yes, you do believe that. Then, can you trust Him to save you? You need to be saved. You can't save yourself. Can you trust Him to save you? "Yes," you answer, "I already do." Well, if you really trust Jesus, then you are definitely saved because you have the only evidence of salvation that all of us have. Other evidences follow after being born again, such as holiness and the fruits of the Spirit, but the only evidence that is the same for everyone is this:

"Nothing in my hands I bring,

Simply to Your cross I cling."

Or even Jack the huckster's words,

"I'm a poor sinner and nothing at all,

But Jesus Christ is my all in all"?

I hope you will mature and grow in experience in many areas, but I don't want you to go any farther than the reason for your evidence and hope. Stop there, and look away from everything that is inside of you or around you to Jesus Christ, and trust His death and suffering on the cross, and to His atonement as your acceptance before God—you are saved. You don't need anything else. You have passed from death to life. *"Whoever believes in him is not condemned"* (John 3:18); *"Whoever believes has eternal life"* (John 6:47).

If I met an angel as I went out of my door, and he said, "Charles Spurgeon, I have come from heaven to tell you that you are forgiven," I would say to him, "I know that without you having to tell me, and on better authority than you have." And if he asked me how I knew it, I would reply, "The Word of God is better to me than the word of an angel, and He has said that *'whoever believes in him is not condemned.'* I do believe in Him, and therefore I am not condemned and I know this without an angel having to tell me so."

Don't be looking after angels, manifestations, evidence, and signs. If you rest on the finished work of Jesus, you already have the best evidence of your salvation in the world. You have God's Word for it, what more do you need? Can't you accept God's Word? You can accept your earthly father's word. You can trust your mother's word, why can't you take God's Word? What immoral hearts we must have to doubt God!

Maybe you say you wouldn't do such a thing. But you doubt God if you don't trust Jesus because *"Whoever does not believe God has made him a liar"* (1 John 5:10). If you don't trust Jesus, then you are saying that God is a liar. You don't want to say that, do you? Believe in the truthfulness of God! May His Spirit bring you to believe the Father's mercy, the power of the Son's blood, and the willingness of the Holy Spirit to bring sinners to Himself!

Read this prayer with me, that you may be led by grace to see that all that you need is in Jesus.

"Prayer is a creature's strength, his very breath and being;

Prayer is the golden key that can open the gate of mercy;

Prayer is the magic sound that said to fate, so be it;

Prayer is the slender nerve that moves the muscles of omnipotence,

So, pray, O creature, for many and great are your wants;

Your mind, your conscience, and your being,

Your needs commend you unto prayer,

The cure of all cares, the grand solution for all pains,

Doubt's destroyer, ruin's remedy, the antidote to all anxieties."

(*A sermon on January 14, 1866, at the Metropolitan Tabernacle, Newington*).

Study Guide

This chapter on the raven's cry really brings home the message of how privileged we, as Christians, are in terms of being able to pray to God. Often, we take it for granted that we are able to speak directly to the Creator.

If you are working through these questions as a group, allow time for any discussions that come from them. If you are on your own, don't rush to answer, but rather use the moment to reflect and see yourself in regards to the topic. Allow the Holy Spirit to lead you and reveal anything that He wants to show you.

1. Do you feel that your prayers are heard? Always, sometimes, or never?
2. Spurgeon uses an interesting argument that because we are capable of sinning, our voice is worth more to God. Do you agree with this statement?
3. In what ways are our cries to God different and more pleasing to God?
4. In point 4, the argument that we have been commanded to pray is made. Do you have trouble obeying such an order? Would it change your thinking if you saw it less as an obligation to fulfill and more as an invitation to respond to?
5. How does grace affect the way that we pray?
6. What does Spurgeon mean when he says we don't pray alone? Who else is praying with us?

3

ORDER AND ARGUMENT IN PRAYER

"Oh, that I knew where I might find him, that I might come even to his seat!
I would lay my case before him and fill my mouth with arguments."
Job 23:3-4

In Job's worst hardships, he cried to the Lord. The longing desire of a child of God in trouble is to see his Father's face one more time. His first prayer is not, "Oh, that I might be healed of the disease which is now in every part of my body!" nor even, "Oh, that I might see my children saved from dying, and my property restored to me from those who would take it!" but the first, main cry is, "Oh, that I might find HIM—who is my God! That I might even come before His throne!"

God's children run home when the storm comes. It's the divine instinct of a Christian to find shelter from all the troubles beneath the wings of Jehovah. *"The Most High, who is my refuge"* (Psalm 91:9) might be a good title for a true believer. A hypocrite, when he feels that he has been hurt or harassed by God, resents it, and like a slave, he will run from the master who has punished him. But the true heir of heaven kisses the hand that struck him and seeks shelter from the whip in the arms of that same God who frowned on him.

You will notice that the desire to find and be with God is intensified by the failure of all our other sources of support and comfort. When Job first saw his friends coming, he might have felt hope that their thoughtful advice and compassionate kindness would take away the sharpness of his grief, but they had not even spoken for long, before he resented their help, and cried out, *"Miserable comforters are you all"* (Job 16:2). They put salt into his wounds, they poured fuel on the flame of his sorrow, they added the sting of their rebuke to his bitter grief. Where they once loved to be in the company of his smile, now they dared to cast shadows on his reputation, which was mean and uncalled for.

It's a terrible thing when a person's wine glass tricks them with the taste of vinegar and their pillow feels like thorns! Job turned away from his friends and looked up to God, just as a traveler leaves his empty bottle and runs as quickly as possible to the source of water. He says goodbye to earthly hopes, and cries to God, *"Oh, that I knew where I might find him"* (Job 23:3).

Nothing teaches us the value and worth of our Creator as much as when we learn that everything else in comparison is empty. *"Cursed is the man who trusts in man and makes flesh his strength"* (Jer 17:5). When the meaning of this verse has really become clear to you, then you will find God's assurance very sweet: *"Blessed is the man who trusts in the Lord, whose trust is the Lord"* (Jer 17:7). Turning away from the 'hives' of what the world offers, where you found many sharp stings and no honey, you will rejoice in Him whose faithful word is sweeter than honey.

We can even see that although a Christian can turn quickly to God in times of trouble, especially when those around him are being hurtful or unkind, sometimes they can't find the comfortable presence of God. This is the worst kind of grief. Our key verse reveals one of Job's deep groans, far deeper than any that came from him because of losing his children and his property, *"Oh, that I knew where I might find him!"* The worst loss of all is to lose the smile of my God. Job had a small taste of the same anguish of Jesus' cry, *"My God, my God, why have you forsaken me?"* (Matt 27:46).

God's presence is always with us in one sense, as He sustains us without being seen, but we don't always enjoy His actual presence. It's like the spouse in the song that is looking for the one they love in their bed at night; they seek but don't find him, and although they stay awake and go through the city they can't locate him. The sad question is asked again and again, *"Have you seen him whom my soul loves?"* (Song 3:3).

You may be loved by God, and yet not know or feel that love in your soul. You may be as dear to His heart as Jesus, and yet for a brief moment He may forsake you, and in a little anger, He may hide Himself from you. But, at such times the desire of the Christian becomes even more intense because God's light is being withheld. Instead of arrogantly saying, "Well, if He leaves me I must do without Him. If I cannot have His comfortable presence I must fight on as best as I can," the heart says, "No, it is my whole life, I must have my God. I die, I sink in deep quicksand where I cannot stand anymore, and nothing but the hand of God can deliver me." The gracious heart speaks with extra passion to find God and sends up its groans, its cries, its sobs and sighs to heaven more frequently and fervently. *"Oh, that I knew where I might find him."*

Distance or effort becomes nothing, if the heart knows where to go, it would quickly overcome the obstacles. It does not care about mountains or rivers, but it would even reach His throne if it knew where to find it. My heart in its desire would break through stone walls, or climb the fortress of heaven to reach God. Even if there were seven hells between me and Him, I would still face the flame if I could reach Him. Nothing would hold me back if I had the chance of standing in His presence and feeling the delight of His love. That seems to be the state of mind Job was in when he said the words we hear.

But we can't stop here on this point, because there is more that we must discuss.

It looks like Job's goal, in desiring the presence of God, was that he might pray to Him. He had prayed, but he wanted to pray in God's presence. He desired to beg and plead before one whom he knew would hear and help him. He longed to state his own case before an impartial Judge. Before the face of the all-wise God, he would appeal from the lower courts, where his friends gave out unrighteous judgment. To the King's Bench—the High Court of heaven—he says, "*I would lay my case before him and fill my mouth with arguments,*" or as some translations say, 'order my cause.'

In this verse, Job teaches us how he meant to plead and intercede with God. He reveals the secrets of his prayer room and unveils the art of prayer. We are admitted into the society of petitioners, we are shown the art and mystery of pleading, we are taught the craft and science of prayer. If we can become apprentices to Job and have a lesson from his Master, we may gain incredible skill in interceding with God.

We can find two things here that are necessary in prayer: Ordering our case, and filling our mouth with arguments. We will look at those two things, and if we learn the lesson, a wonderful result will follow.

Our Case Must Be Ordered Before God

There is a foolish idea that prayer is a very easy thing, a common duty that can be done in any way, without thought or effort. Some think that you only have to take a book down and get through a certain number of beautifully written words, and you have prayed and can put the book away again. Others suppose that to use a book is traditional and that you should rather say spontaneous words, sentences that come to your mind in a rush, like a herd of pigs or a pack of dogs, and that when you have said them, understanding some of what you have said, you have prayed.

Now, none of these forms of prayer were used by Christians from long ago. They appear to have thought much more seriously about prayer than many of us do these days. It seems to have been an important duty for them, an exercise they practiced, in which some of them became well-known, and were blessed in it. They reaped great harvests in the field of prayer and found the mercy seat to be filled with incredible treasures.

Those Christians were accustomed, just like Job, to order their case before God. They were like a petitioner who doesn't come into court thinking that he can state his case on the spur of the moment, but enters in with his lawsuit well prepared, having learned how he needs to behave in the presence of the great One to whom he is appealing. It is good to approach the King of kings with premeditation and preparation, knowing what we are about, where we are standing, and what it is we want to obtain. In times of hardship and worry, we may rush to God just as we are, like the dove as it flies into the cleft of the rock, even though her feathers are ruffled. But in ordinary times we shouldn't come with an unprepared spirit, the same way that a child doesn't come to his father in the morning until he has dressed and washed his face.

Imagine a priest that has a sacrifice to offer. He does not rush into the court of the priests and hack at the bull with the first ax that he can lay his hand on. Instead, when he gets up, he washes his feet at the bronze basin, puts on his priestly garments, then comes to the altar with his offering properly divided according to the law. He is careful to do everything exactly according to the command, even down to the smallest details of placing the fat, the liver, and the kidneys. Then he takes the blood in a bowl and pours it in an appropriate place at the foot of the altar, not throwing it wherever he thinks might be best. He doesn't use a common flame on the fire but uses the sacred fire from the altar.

Now this ritual is all done away with, but the truth it can teach us remains the same: our spiritual sacrifices should be offered with holy care. Our prayer should not be leaping out of our bed, kneeling down, and saying the first thing that comes to our minds. On the contrary, we must wait on the Lord with holy fear and sacred awe.

See how David prayed when God had blessed him—he went in before the Lord. He did not stand outside at a distance, but he went in before the Lord and he sat down—for sitting is not a bad posture for prayer, no matter what some might say—and sitting down quietly and calmly before the Lord he began to pray, but not until he had first thought over God's goodness, and so reached a spirit of prayer. Then with the assistance of the Holy Spirit, he opened his mouth.

We should seek the Lord in this style more often! Abraham is a great example for us: he got up early—here we see his willingness. He took a three-day journey—here we see his determination. He left his servants at the bottom of the hill —here we see his privacy. He carried the wood and the fire with him—here we see his preparation. And last of all, he built the altar and laid the wood in order, and then took the knife—here we see the devoted care of his worship.

David puts it this way, *"In the morning I prepare a sacrifice for you and watch"* (Psalm 5:3), which means that he ordered his thoughts like men of war, or that he aimed his prayers like arrows. He did not take the arrow and put it on the bowstring and shoot and shoot, and shoot anywhere. Instead, after he had taken out the chosen shaft, and fitted it to the string, he took deliberate aim. He looked—looked well—at the target, kept his eyes fixed on it, directing his prayer, and then drew his bow with all his strength and let the arrow fly. Then, when the shaft had left his hand, what does he do? He watches.

He looked to see where the arrow went, to see what effect it had, because he expected an answer to his prayers, and was not as many of us who hardly think of our prayers after we have said them. David knew that he had a duty in front of him that required all his mental powers, he ordered his senses and went about the work in a work-like manner, as one who believed and meant to succeed in it.

We should plow carefully and pray carefully. The better the work, the more attention it deserves. To be anxious in the shop but not care what happens in the prayer room is almost like blasphemy because we are insinuating that anything is alright for God, but the world must have our best.

Unfortunately, if you want to know what order we should follow in prayer, I am not about to give you a scheme like those that many have drawn up, where adoration, confession, petition, intercession, and ascription are arranged in sequence. I don't agree that any kind of order like that carries any Godly authority. I have not been referring to any routine order, because our prayers will be acceptable and proper in any form, for there are examples of prayers, in all shapes, in the Old and New Testament. I think the true spiritual order of prayer consists of something more than simply arranging it correctly.

The right place for us to start is to first feel that we are doing something that is real. We must know that we are about to address God; whom we cannot see, but who is present; whom we cannot touch or hear, or realize through our senses, but who is with us if we were speaking to a real flesh-and-blood friend like ourselves. Once we feel the reality of God's presence, our mind will be led by grace into humility; we will feel like Abraham, when he said, *"I have undertaken to speak to the Lord, I who am but dust and ashes"* (Gen 18:27).

Consequently, we will not enter into prayer like children repeating their school lessons through rote learning. We will not speak as if we were rabbis instructing our pupils or as thieves stopping a person and demanding their money and belongings. Instead, we will be humble, yet bold petitioners, humbly asking for mercy through the Savior's blood. We will not have the attitude of a slave but the loving reverence of a child; not a rude, demanding child, but a teachable, obedient child, that honors his Father, and sincerely asks, but in submission to his Father's will.

When I feel that I am in the presence of God, and take my rightful position there, the next thing I will want to accept is that I have no right to what I am asking, and cannot expect to receive it except as a gift of grace. I need to remember that God limits the means by which He gives me mercy—He will give it to me through His Son. So, let me bring myself under the Redeemer's approval. Let me feel that it is no longer I who am speaking but Christ that is speaking with me and that while I plead, I plead His wounds, His life, His death, His blood, Himself. This is what it means to get into order.

The next thing is to consider what I am going to ask for. It is a good thing, when praying, to begin making specific and definite requests. Many of the loud, public prayers we hear are from people who are not really asking God for anything. I must admit that I have prayed this way myself, and have heard many prayers like this where I didn't feel that anything was asked from God—a lot of excellent doctrinal and experiential words were said uttered, but hardly any real requests, and even then, the request was vague, chaotic and had no order. I believe that prayer should be specific, asking for something definitely and distinctly because your mind has realized its specific need for that thing, and so you must beg for it.

It is good not to beat around the bush in prayer, but to come directly to the point. I like that prayer of Abraham's, *"Oh that Ishmael might live before you!"* (Gen 17:18). We can clearly see the name and the person being prayed for, and the blessing that is desired, all in just a few words—"Ishmael might live before you." Many people would probably have used a roundabout way of bringing this prayer before the Lord, "Oh that our beloved child might be regarded with the favor which You give to those who," etc. Why not just say "Ishmael," if you mean "Ishmael," put it in plain words before the Lord. Some people can't even pray for the pastor without using such meandering adjectives that you would think it was some kind of saint or a great man of God, or someone that mentioning too specifically would be a let-down. Why not be to-the-point, and say what we mean as well as mean what we say?

Ordering our case would make us more specific in our minds. It is not necessary to ask for every good thing you can think of. It is also not necessary to itemize the catalog of everything that you may need, want, have had, can have, or shall have. Ask for what you need now. As a rule, stick to the present need, ask for your daily bread—what you want now—ask for that. Ask for it clearly, as you are before God who does not care for your exquisite expressions, and who sees your eloquence and speech as nothing but vanity. You are before the Lord, let your words be few, but let your heart be passionate.

The ordering of prayer is not quite completed when you have asked for what you want through Jesus Christ—there is more. We should also examine what we are asking for, to see if it's really the right thing, for some prayers would never be offered if people just thought about them first. A little consideration about what we are asking would show us that what we desire might be better left alone.

We might even have a hidden motive in our desire which is not Christ-like, a selfish reason, that forgets God's glory and only looks out for our own ease and comfort. Now, although we may ask for things that are for our good, we must still never let that interfere with the glory of God in any way. Combined with acceptable prayer we should find the holy salt of submission to God's will.

I like what Luther said, "Lord, I will have my will of You at this time." Now, why would I like an expression like that? It's because it is followed by the next words, which say, "I will have my will, for I know that my will is Your will." Without the last words, it would have been an evil, selfish arrogance, but as a whole, it is a wonderful motto.

When we are sure that what we ask for is for God's glory, then, if we have power in prayer, we can say, *"I will not let you go unless you bless me"* (Gen 32:26). We might have very personal, face-to-face dealings with God, and like Jacob with the angel, we may even wrestle and try to find a way to get the upper hand sooner than be sent away without the blessing. But we must be very clear, before we come to that place, that what we are seeking is really for the Master's honor.

Put these three things together: The deep spirituality that sees prayer as being a real conversation with the invisible God; the reality of prayer in being specific, asking for what we know we want; and with passion, believing the thing to be necessary, and so taking hold of it in complete submission, leaving it with the Master's will—combine all of these, and you have a clear idea of what it means to order your case before the Lord.

But remember, prayer itself is an art that only the Holy Spirit can teach us. He is the giver of all prayer. Pray for prayer—pray until you can pray, pray to be helped to pray, and don't give up praying because you can't pray, because it is when you think you can't pray that you are praying the most. Sometimes, when you have no comfort in your requests, that is when your broken, cast-down heart is really wrestling and truly pushing in with the Most High.

Filling the Mouth with Arguments

Next, we will see that prayer is not filling the mouth with words, good phrases, or pretty expressions, but filling the mouth with arguments. The Christians of old were known to argue in prayer. When we come to the gate of mercy, strong arguments are the knocks that open it.

The first question we must ask is, why should arguments be used at all? The answer we find is that it's not because God is slow to give, or that we can change the divine purpose, nor because God needs to be informed of any circumstance about ourselves or anything in connection with the mercy asked. The arguments are for our own benefit not for His. He wants us to plead and beg Him, and to bring our strong reasons forward, because, as Isaiah said, this will show that we feel the value of the mercy. When a man looks to argue for something it's because he sees that which he is seeking as important.

Again, our use of arguments teaches us the foundation on which we obtain the blessing. If we come with an argument of our own merit, we would never succeed; a successful argument is always founded on grace, and so, the heart that pleads begins to understand that it is by grace, and by grace alone, that a sinner gains anything from the Lord. Besides, the use of arguments is intended to stir up our passion and intensity. If we use one argument with God, we will build up more momentum and power in the next one and will find even more strength in the one after that, and the one that follows that one, too.

The best prayers I have ever heard in our prayer meetings have been those that have been full of arguments. Sometimes my heart has melted as I have listened to fellow Christians who have come before God feeling that they really needed mercy and that they must have it. First, they pleaded with God to give it for this reason, and then for a second, and then for a third, and then for a fourth and a fifth, until they stirred up the passion and urgency of all those gathered there.

There's no need for prayer at all as far as God is concerned, but how necessary it is for us on our own account! If we were not compelled to pray, I wonder if we could even live as Christians. If God's mercies came to us without us having to ask for them, they wouldn't be half as useful as they are to us now, when they have to be sought for, because now we get a double blessing; a blessing in obtaining it, and a blessing in seeking it. The very act of prayer is a blessing.

To pray is like bathing in a cool gentle stream, and escaping from the heat of the summer sun. To pray is like mounting on an eagle's wings above the clouds and getting into heaven where God is. It is like entering the treasure house of God and enriching yourself from an inexhaustible store. Praying is grasping heaven in your arms, embracing God within your heart, and feeling your body as a temple of the Holy Spirit. Apart from the answer, prayer is a blessing. It is throwing off your burdens, tearing away your rags, shaking off your diseases, being filled with spiritual strength, and reaching the highest point of Christian health. God help us in the art of arguing with God in prayer.

Here is the most interesting part, a short summary, and a list of some of the arguments that have been successful with God. A full list would require an essay that someone like John Owen could write.

It's good to ask according to Jehovah's character and abilities. Abraham did so when he was looking for God's justice. He was begging for Sodom, and says, *"Suppose there are fifty righteous within the city. Will you then sweep away the place and not spare it for the fifty righteous who are in it? Far be it from you to do such a thing, to put the righteous to death with the wicked, so that the righteous fare as the wicked! Far be that from you! Shall not the Judge of all the earth do what is just?"* (Gen 18:24-25).

Here the struggle begins. It was a powerful argument that Abraham used to reach the Lord's left hand, and interrupted it just when the thunderbolt was about to fall. But there was also a reply. Abraham was informed that his intervention would not spare the city. We see that when he was up against a wall, he didn't give up, but stepped back slightly. When he realized he would not get the justice he was seeking, he reached for God's right hand of mercy. That gave him a great foothold when he asked if the city might be spared for ten righteous people.

So you and I can also take hold of the justice, mercy, faithfulness, wisdom, patience, kindness of God, and we'll find each of His characteristics to be a battering ram that can open the gates of heaven.

Another incredible weapon in the battle of prayer is God's promise. When Jacob was on the other side of the River Jabbok, and his brother Esau was coming with armed men, he begged God not to allow Esau to destroy the women and the children. The main reason he used in his argument was, *"But you said, 'I will surely do you good'"* (Gen 32:12). The strength of that request is amazing! He was holding God to His word, *"But you said."* The character of God is a great horn of the altar to grab onto, but the promise, which has the character and more in it, is an even mightier hold. *"But you said."*

Remember the way David said it. After Nathan had spoken the promise, David added to the end of his prayer the words, *"Do as you have spoken"* (2 Sam 7:25). That is a legitimate argument for every honest man: He said it, and will He not do it? *"Let God be true though every one were a liar"* (Rom 3:4). Isn't He true? Won't He keep His word? Won't every word that comes out of His lips stand strong and be fulfilled? Solomon, at the opening of the temple, used the same mighty plea. He asks God to remember the word that He had spoken to his father David and to bless that place.

When someone gives a legal letter to pay, their honor is engaged. They sign, and then must carry it out when the time comes, or else he loses credit. God never dishonors His bills. The credit of the Most High has never been challenged, and never shall be. He is punctual, not early, and never late. You can search through the Bible, and compare it with the experience of God's people, and the two balance out from beginning to end, with many of the great men of faith agreeing with Joshua in saying, *"Not one word of all the good promises that the Lord had made to the house of Israel had failed; all came to pass"* (Josh 21:45).

If you have been given a promise from God, you don't need to ask with an 'if' in it; you can plead with certainty. If God has given His word for the mercy that you are asking for, there isn't much room to question His will. You know His will; that will is in the promise, plead it. Don't let Him rest until He fulfills it. He means to fulfill it, or else He would not have given it. God doesn't give His word to keep us quiet and to keep us hopeful for a while, with the intention of putting us off at the last moment. When He speaks, He speaks because He means to act.

A third argument to be used is the one employed by Moses, the great man of God. How forcefully he argued with God at one time in this regard! *"Lest the land from which you brought us say, 'Because the Lord was not able to bring them into the land that he promised them, and because he hated them, he has brought them out to put them to death in the wilderness'"* (Deut 9:28). There are some occasions when the name of God is closely tied to the history of His people. Sometimes in relying on His promise, Christians will have to take a certain course of action. Now, if the Lord is not as good as His promise, not only are we as Christians deceived, but the wicked world would say, "Aha! Where is your God?"

Look at the case of Mr. Muller from Bristol. For many years he declared that God hears prayer, and stood firm in that conviction, going on to build many houses as orphanages. I suppose that, if he needed to feed and look after the many children in these homes, he could have used the argument,

"What will you do for your great name?" (Josh 7:9). And for us, when we are in trouble and have received the promise, we can say, "Lord, You have said, You will *'deliver you from six troubles; in seven no evil shall touch you'* (Job 5:19). I have told my friends and neighbors that I put my trust in You, and if You do not deliver me now, where is Your name? God, come and do this thing, otherwise, Your honor will be thrown into the dust."

Added to this, we can use the argument of the harsh things said by those who criticized God. Hezekiah did this so well when he took Rabshakeh's letter and placed it before the Lord. How would that help, when it was full of blasphemy? *"Do not listen to Hezekiah when he misleads you by saying, 'The Lord will deliver us.' Has any of the gods of the nations ever delivered his land out of the hand of the king of Assyria? Where are the gods of Hamath and Arpad? Where are the gods of Sepharvaim, Hena, and Ivvah? Have they delivered Samaria out of my hand? Who among all the gods of the lands have delivered their lands out of my hand, that the Lord should deliver Jerusalem out of my hand?"* (2 Kings 18:32-35). Does that have any effect? Yes! It was a blessing that Rabshakeh wrote that letter because it provoked the Lord to help His people.

Sometimes Christians can rejoice when they see their enemies lose control, get angry, and criticize God. "Now, they have criticized the Lord Himself, and not just attacked me, but the Most High." It's no longer the poor, insignificant Hezekiah with his little band of soldiers, but it is Jehovah, the King of angels, who has come to fight against Rabshakeh. What will you do now, arrogant soldier of proud

Sennacherib? Won't you be completely destroyed when Jehovah Himself has entered into the battle?

All the progress that has been made by religious organizations, all the wrong things said by speculative atheists and others, should be used by Christians as an argument for God as to why He should help the Gospel. "Lord, see how they are attacking the Gospel of Jesus! Lift Your right hand! They are defying You, God! The Antichrist has set itself up in the place where Your Son was once honored and instead of the Gospel being preached from the pulpits, organized religion is now declared. Arise, O God, wake up and let Your sacred passion burn! Your old enemy is winning. See the prostitute of Babylon on her scarlet-colored beast riding in victory! Come, Jehovah! Come, Jehovah, and show what Your hand can do!" This is a legitimate form of pleading with God, for His great name's sake.

We can also plead with the sorrow of His people. This is often done. Jeremiah is the great master of this art. He says, *"The precious sons of Zion, worth their weight in fine gold, how they are regarded as earthen pots, the work of a potter's hands!"* *"Her princes were purer than snow, whiter than milk; their bodies were more ruddy than coral, the beauty of their form was like sapphire. Now their face is blacker than soot"* (Lam 4:2,7-8). He talks of all their griefs and difficulties in the siege. He calls on the Lord to see the suffering of Zion, and before long his cries were heard.

There is nothing as eloquent for a father as his child's cry. There is one thing still stronger than that: a moan. When the child is so sick that it cannot cry anymore, and lies moaning with a moan that shows extreme suffering and intense weakness, who can resist it? And when Israel was brought so low that they could hardly cry, only their moans were heard, the Lord's time of deliverance came, and He showed that He loves His people. Whenever you are also in the same condition, you can also plead with moans. When you see a church brought low you can use its grief as an argument for God to return and save the remnant of His people.

It's good to plead with God using the past as an argument. Those of you who are experienced Christians, know how to do this. Here is David's example: *"O you who have been my help. Cast me not off; forsake me not"* (Psalm 27:9). He pleads for God's mercy from when he was young. He speaks of being chosen by God from when he was born, and then he pleads, *"So even to old age and gray hairs, O God, do not forsake me"* (Psalm 71:18). When Moses speaks, he also says, *"Your people, whom you brought up out of the land of Egypt"* (Ex 32:7). It's as if he would say, "Don't leave Your work unfinished, You have begun to build, complete it. You have fought the first battle, Lord, end the campaign! Go on until You get a complete victory."

How often have we cried in our trouble, "Lord, You did deliver me in that difficult time, when it seemed as if no help was near. You have never forsaken me yet. I have set up my Ebenezer in Your name—a commemoration stone of the help you gave" (1 Samuel 7:12). If You had intended to leave me, why have You showed me such things? Have You brought Your servant to this place to put him to shame?" We deal with a God who never changes; who will do in the future what He has done in the past because He never turns from

His purpose, and cannot be sidetracked in His design. SO, the past becomes a powerful way to win blessings from Him.

We can even use our own unworthiness as an argument with God. *"Out of the eater came something to eat. Out of the strong came something sweet"* (Judges 14:14). In one place, David begs, *"O Lord, pardon my guilt, for it is great"* (Psalm 25:11). That is an extraordinary form of reasoning, but being interpreted it means, "Lord, why should You go about doing little things? You are a great God, and here is a great sinner—an appropriate vessel to show Your grace. The greatness of my sin makes me a platform for the greatness of Your mercy. Let the greatness of Your love be seen in me."

Moses seems to have the same thing on his mind when he asks God to show His power in sparing His sinful people, and God's restraint is incredible. There is such a thing as crouching low before the throne and crying, "Oh God, don't break me—I am a bruised reed. Don't tread on my little life, it is only a smoldering wick. Will You hunt me? Will You come out, as David said, 'after a dead dog, after a flea?' Will you pursue me like a leaf that is blown in the storm? Will you watch me, as Job said, as though I were a vast sea or a great whale? No, but because I am so little, and because the greatness of Your mercy can be shown in someone as insignificant and evil as me, therefore, O God, have mercy on me."

Once, God made a successful plea for Elijah. When the prophet had asked his opponents to see if their god could answer them by fire, you can probably guess the excitement that must have been in his mind. With sarcasm, he said, *"Cry aloud: for he is a god; Either he is musinging, or he is relieving himself, or he is on a journey, or perhaps he is asleep and must be awakened"* (1 Kings 18:27). As they cut themselves with knives and leaped on the altar, Elijah must have looked down on their useless efforts and cries with mockery!

But think of how his heart must have pounded, if it had not been for the strength of his faith, when he repaired the altar of God that was broken down, put the wood in place, and killed the bull. He could have cried something like, "Pour water on it. You won't catch me hiding fire; pour water on the sacrifice." When they had done so, he told them to do it a second time, and they did. Then he said they must do it a third time. When it was all covered with water, soaked and saturated, he stood up and cried to God, *"Let it be known this day that you are God in Israel"* (1 Kings 18:36).

Here everything was put to the test. Jehovah's own existence was at stake, before the eyes of everyone by this bold prophet. But the prophet was heard! Down came the fire and devoured not only the sacrifice, but the wood, the stones, and even the water that was in the trenches, for Jehovah God had answered His servant's prayer. Sometimes we can do the same, and say to Him, "By Your existence, if You really are God, show Yourself to help Your people!"

Finally, the best Christian argument to use in prayer is the sufferings, death, merit, and intercession of Jesus. I am worried that we don't understand the power that we have when we are allowed to plead with God for Jesus' sake. I only thought about this recently, it was quite new to me, but I am sure it should not have been new, that I should've known this all along. When we ask God to hear us, using Jesus' name, we usually mean, "Oh Lord, Your own Son deserves this from You, do this for me because of what He merits." But if we knew it we might go farther.

Imagine you told me that you had a warehouse in the city, "Sir, come to my office, and use my name, and say that they must give you the thing you are needing." I could go in, use your name, and get what I was after as a matter of right and necessity. This is exactly what Jesus says to us. "If you need anything from God, all that the Father has belongs to Me, go and use My name."

Imagine you gave someone your checkbook signed with your own name and left blank, to be filled in as they wanted, that would almost be what Jesus has done when He said, *"If you ask me anything in my name, I will do it"* (John 14:14). If I had a reputable name at the bottom of a check, I would cash it at the bank. It's the same when you have got Jesus' name; God's justice is indebted to it, and its merits have a claim on the Most High. When you have Jesus' name, there is no need to speak with fear, worry, or be nervous. Don't doubt or let your faith slip! When you plead the name of Christ, you plead in a name that shakes the gates of hell, and which the angels obey, and God feels the holy power of that request.

It would be better if we thought more of Jesus' grief and suffering in our prayers. Bring His wounds before God; remind Him of Jesus' cries and groans from Gethsemane, and let His blood from Calvary speak for itself. Tell God that with such grief, cries, and groans to plead, you can't be denied or rejected. Arguments like these will make sure of it.

We Will Have Our Mouths Filled with Praises

If the Holy Spirit will teach us how to order our case, and how to fill our mouth with arguments, then the result will be that our mouths will fill with praise for God. Someone whose mouth is full of arguments in prayer will soon have their mouth full of blessings in answer to prayer.

What is your mouth full of? Is it full of complaining? Pray that God will rinse that out of your mouth, because it will do nothing for you, only make your stomach and heart bitter. Let your mouth be full of prayer, full of it, full of arguments so that there is no room for anything else. Then go with this wonderful mouthful, and you will soon come away with whatever you have asked of God. Just delight yourself in Him, and He will give you the desire of your heart.

I am not entirely sure, but the meaning of the verse, *"Open your mouth wide, and I will fill it"* (Psalm 81:10), might have originated from Oriental customs. Apparently, the King of Persia ordered the chief of his nobility, who had done something incredible, to open his mouth. When he had opened it, the king began to put pearls, diamonds, rubies, and emeralds into his mouth, until he had filled it as much as possible, and then let him go. Only those who were favorites in the Oriental Courts were granted this privilege.

Whether that is the origin or explanation of the verse or not, it is still a wonderful picture to describe it. God says, "Open your mouth with arguments," and then He will fill it with priceless mercies and riches of unspeakable value. Wouldn't you open your mouth wide if it was going to be filled like that? Surely you don't need to be extremely clever to see the benefits of it.

So, let us open our mouths wide when we have to plead with God. Our needs are great, let the way and manner we ask be great, then the reward will also be great. You are not poor in Him, you are poor in your stomach. May God give you 'large-mouthedness' in prayer, great power, not in the kind of language you use, but in using the right arguments.

What I have been saying here to us as Christians, also applies in the same measure to those who are not born again. May God open your eyes to see the power of it, and to rise up in humble prayer to the Lord Jesus Christ and find eternal life in Him.

(*A sermon on July 15, 1866, at the Metropolitan Tabernacle, Newington*).

Study Guide

It's very helpful to use a notebook when working through these questions to keep a record of ideas, thoughts, and personal reflections. In this way, you can refer back and see things that you are struggling with, allow the Lord to deal with them, or even be surprised to find how you have grown in certain areas. It is also a great way to help you focus on the study guide, as writing down answers often helps to store information much more than just giving a quick verbal response.

1. Spurgeon looks at the difference between turning to the world and turning to God by using the verse Jeremiah 17:5. Have you ever had an experience like this?
2. The idea that prayer should be ordered and not 'Off-the-cuff' or haphazard might seem a bit regimental and lacking in grace. What is your view on this?
3. What is the difference between arguing with God and presenting our arguments?
4. There is a list of different arguments that can be used in prayer with God. Which, if any, have you used when coming before God with requests?
5. Do you find it easier to complain to God or sing His praises?
6. Do you agree with the statement, "Someone whose mouth is full of arguments in prayer will soon have their mouth full of blessings in answer to prayer"?

4

PLEADING

"But I am poor and needy; hasten to me, O God! You are my help and my deliverer; O Lord, do not delay!"
Psalm 70:5

Long ago, young painters were desperate to study under the great masters. They realized that the easiest way to do this was if they entered the schools of these experts. Today, we will pay huge fees so that our children can be taught or schooled by those who are specialists in their professions and trades. If any of us want to learn the sacred art and mystery of prayer, it would be good for us to study under the greatest masters.

I can't find anyone who understood this better than the psalmist, David. He was so good at knowing how to praise, that his psalms have been used, quoted, and spoken by good people since his time. He also understood how to pray so well, that if we catch his spirit, and follow his way of praying, we will have learned to plead with God after the best-recognized example. First of all, look at Jesus, David's descendant, and Lord, that most incredible of all intercessors; next to Him, you will find David to be one of the greatest models to copy.

So, we will look at the verse from Psalms 70 as the product of a great master in spiritual matters, and we will study it, praying that God will help us to pray as David did.

In the verse, we see the heart of a successful prayer in four aspects. First, we have the heart confessing, "I am poor and needy." Next, we have the heart pleading from its sorry state, and adds, "Hasten to me, O God!" Third, we come across a determined heart, for it cries, "Hasten to me," and then says the same thing again in a different way, "Do not delay." And lastly, in the fourth view, we see a heart reaching for God, because the psalmist says, "You are my help and my deliverer." With both hands, the heart takes hold of its God, and will not let Him go until it receives a blessing.

A Confessing Heart

Looking at our model of prayer, we start with a soul that confesses.

Before a wrestler enters the ring, he must strip and take off all unnecessary clothes. Confession is the same for us when we are about to plead with God. A sprinter on the racetrack of prayer cannot hope to win unless he puts off every hindrance of sin through confession, repentance, and faith.

Now, we must remember that confession is absolutely necessary for sinners when they first seek a Savior. It is not possible for you to find peace for your troubled heart until you have acknowledged your sin and iniquity before the Lord. You can do what you want, even attempt to believe in Jesus, but you will find that the faith of a Christian is not in you unless you are willing to make a full confession of your transgression, and open your heart before God. We don't usually think of giving charity to people that don't need it, the doctor doesn't give medicine to those who are not sick.

There is more than enough work for us to do without having to take on extra, unnecessary tasks. Clothing those who are not naked, and feeding those who are not hungry, is unproductive, and won't bring us any credit. God will not waste His time like this. You must be empty before you can be filled by Him, and you must confess your emptiness, too, because He will not come to fill the full, or lift up those who are already high enough in their own eyes.

The blind man in the Bible had to feel his blindness, and sit by the road begging. If he had entertained a doubt as to whether he was blind or not, the Lord would have passed him by. Jesus opens the eyes of those who confess their blindness, but for others, He says, *"Now that you say, 'We see,' your guilt remains"* (John 9:41). He asks those who were brought to Him, *"What do you want me to do for you?"* (Mark 10:51) so that their need may be made public. It is the same for us; we must confess, or we cannot get the blessing.

For those who really desire to find peace with God, and salvation through the precious blood, it will be good if your confession before God is honest, very sincere, and very explicit. You should have nothing to hide because there is nothing that you can hide. He knows your guilt already, but He wants you to know it, and so He tells you to confess it.

Go into all the details of your sin in your secret admissions before God, strip yourself of all excuses, make no apologies, say, *"Against you, you only, have I sinned and done what is evil in your sight, so that you may be justified in your words and blameless in your judgment"* (Psalm 51:4). Admit the evil of sin, ask God to make you feel it, do not treat it as nothing, for it is not. To redeem the sinner from the effect of sin, Jesus has to die, and unless you are delivered from it you must die eternally.

So, don't play with sin, don't confess it as if it was some excusable fault, which would not have been noticed unless God had been so harsh. Instead, make every effort to see sin the way God sees it, as an offense against all that is good, a rebellion against all that is kind, see it as treason, an ingratitude towards God, a very low and evil thing.

Don't think that you can improve your condition before God by painting your case in brighter colors than it should be. Paint it as dark as possible, but even that is not enough. When you feel your sin the most, you won't even have felt half of it, when you confess it as fully as you can, you won't know a tenth of it. But, to the best of your ability, admit it all and come clean. Say, *"I have sinned against heaven and before you"* (Luke 15:21). Acknowledge the sins of your childhood and your adulthood, the sins of your body and your heart, the sins you didn't plan and the ones you did, sins against the law, and offenses against the Gospel. Admit them all. Don't try to deny even the smallest part of the evil that God's law, your own conscience, and His Holy Spirit have rightfully charged you.

If you want peace and approval with God in prayer, confess what your sin deserves. Submit to whatever sentence God hands down for you to endure, confess that the deepest part of hell is what you rightfully deserve. Don't just confess this with your mouth, but with your heart as well. Let this be the sad song of your heart:

"Should sudden vengeance seize my breath,

I must pronounce You just in death;

And, if my soul were sent to hell,

Your righteous law approves it well."

IF YOU WILL CONDEMN YOURSELF, God will clear your name. If you put the rope around your neck and sentence yourself, then the One who should have sentenced you will say, "I forgive you, through the merit of My Son." But don't expect the King of heaven to forgive a traitor if he will not confess and give up his treason. Even the most loving father expects his child to humble himself when he has done wrong, and he won't give in until the child has cried and said, "Father, I have sinned."

Do you expect God to humble Himself to you? Would He do that without bringing you to humble yourself to Him? Do you think He will ignore your faults and pretend your transgressions are not there? He will have mercy, but He must be holy; He is ready to forgive, but not to tolerate sin, and therefore, He cannot let you be forgiven if you embrace your sins, or if you say, "I have not sinned." Be quick then, to bow before the mercy seat and say, "I am poor and needy, I am sinful, I am lost, have pity on me." You will start your prayer in the right way with such an acknowledgment, and through Jesus, you will succeed in it.

The same principle applies to us as Christians. We are praying for a move of the Holy Spirit's power in our churches, and to make this request successful, it's necessary for us all to confess this as the verse says, *"I am poor and needy"* (Psalm 109:22). We must realize in this situation, we are powerless. Salvation comes from Jesus and we cannot save a single person. The Spirit of God is in Jesus, and we must seek Him as the Head of the church. We cannot tell the Spirit what to do, and yet we can't do anything without Him. He blows where He wants. We must feel this and admit it. Will you agree to this right now? Will you confess this in your heart?

We must also acknowledge that we are not worthy for the Holy Spirit to come down and work with us and by us. There is nothing good or worthy in us for His purpose, except that He will make us worthy. Our sins might make Him leave us. He has worked with us, been tender towards us, but He might go away and say, "I will not shine on that church anymore, and not bless that ministry any longer." We must feel our unworthiness; it is good preparation for sincere, honest prayer. God will have His church before He blesses it, and the blessing will be from Him and not from us. *"Not by might, nor by power, but by my Spirit, says the Lord"* (Zech 4:6).

The story of Gideon was a remarkable one, and it began with two very clear signs. I think God would want all of us to learn the same lesson that He taught Gideon, and when we have mastered that lesson, He will use us for His own purposes. You will remember that Gideon laid a fleece on the ground, and in the morning all around it was dry and only the fleece was wet. It was God who saturated the fleece so that Gideon had to squeeze all the water out, and the moisture was not because it had been placed somewhere to aid it in getting wet, for all around it was dry.

He wants us to learn that if the dew of His grace fills us with heavenly moisture, it's not because we lie on the ground of a ministry that God usually blesses, or because we are in a church which the Lord graciously visits, but we must be made to see that when the Holy Spirit visits us, it is a fruit of God's grace, and a gift of His love, and has nothing to do with man or his will.

But then the miracle was reversed. Thomas Fuller said, "God's miracles will bear to be turned inside out and look as glorious one way as another." The next night, the fleece was dry, and all around was wet. Skeptics might have said, "Yes, but a fleece would naturally attract moisture, and if there was any in the air, it would be absorbed by the wool." However, on this occasion, the dew was not where it should have been, even though it was all around. The ground was damp and the fleece was dry.

So, God wants us to know that He doesn't give us His grace because of any natural qualifications that we have to receive it, and even when He gives us a heart that is prepared to receive it, He wants us to understand that His grace and Spirit are free to act without limits and that He doesn't work according to any of our rules we have made. If the fleece must be wet, He pours dew on it, not because it's a fleece, but because He chooses to do so. He will have all the glory of all His grace from beginning to end.

So, come and be followers of this truth. Consider that every good and perfect gift must come from the great Father of lights. We are His creation, He must work all our works in us. Grace is not to be commanded by our position or condition, the wind blows where it wants, the Lord works and no man can stop Him, but if He doesn't work, then the strongest and the most committed efforts will be in vain.

It's very significant that before Jesus fed the thousands, He made the disciples count all their provisions. It was good to let them see how low their supplies had become, because then when the crowds were fed they could not say the basket had fed them, nor that the boy had done it. God wants us to feel how little our bread loaves and how small our fishes are, and compel us to ask the question, *"What are they for so many?"* (John 6:9).

When Jesus told the disciples to throw the net over the right side of the boat, and they dragged such a mighty shoal back to the land, He didn't perform the miracle until they had confessed that they had worked all through the night and had caught nothing. So, they were taught that the success of their fishing expedition was dependent on the Lord, and that it was not their net, the way they had dragged it, nor their skill and art in handling their boats, but that their success came completely from their Lord. We must grab hold of this truth, and the sooner we come to it the better.

Before the Jews kept the Passover festival, observe what they did. The unleavened bread was to be brought in, and the lamb was to be eaten, but there could not be any unleavened bread or lamb until they had got rid of all the old leaven from the dough. If you have any old strength and self-confidence, if you have anything that is your own, and is 'leavened,' it must be thrown out. There must be an empty cupboard before any heavenly provision can be put inside of it, on which the spiritual Passover can be kept. I thank God when He cleans us out, I bless His name when He brings us to feel the poverty of our hearts as a church, for then the blessing will definitely come.

Another illustration will show this even more clearly. Let's take a look at Elijah with the priests of Baal at Carmel. The test to decide Israel's choice was this—the God that answers by fire would be the real God. Baal's priests called down flame from heaven in vain. Elijah was confident that it would only come down on his sacrifice, but he was also determined to make sure that the false priests and the fickle people would know that he himself had not somehow produced the fire.

He set out to make it clear that there was no human interference, trickery, or anything to dispute the matter. The flame needed to be seen as coming from God alone. Remember the prophet's serious command, *"'Fill four jars with water and pour it on the burnt offering and on the wood.' And he said, 'Do it a second time.' And they did it a second time. And he said, 'Do it a third time.' And they did it a third time. And the water ran around the altar and filled the trench also with water"* (1 Kings 18:33-35).

There was no way that any dormant fires were still there. If there had been anything combustible or any hidden chemicals that could start a fire the way cheaters did in those days, all of it would have been soaked and damaged.

When he had done enough so that it was impossible to imagine anyone being able to burn the sacrifice, then the prophet lifted his eyes up to heaven and began to plead, and the fire of the Lord came down, consuming the burnt sacrifice and the wood, the altar stones, and the dust, and even burned up the water that was in the trench. Then when all the people saw it they bowed down, and they said, *"The Lord, he is God; the Lord, he is God"* (1 Kings 18:39).

If God wants to richly bless us in the church, He might send us the trial of pouring water once, twice, and even three times. He might discourage us, grieve us, test us, and bring us low until we all can see that it is not because of the preacher, it is not the organization, or because of man, but completely of God, the Alpha and the Omega, who works all things according to the counsel of His will.

So, I have shown us that for a successful season of prayer, the best place to start is confessing that we are poor and needy.

A Pleading Heart

Secondly, after the heart has unburdened itself of all weights of merit and self-sufficiency, it can then begin to pray. That is when we find a heart that pleads.

"But I am poor and needy; hasten to me, O God! You are my help and my deliverer; O Lord, do not delay!" If we are observant, we can find four different pleas in this single verse.

On this topic I would say that it is a habit of faith, when praying, to use pleas. People who just say prayers, and do not really pray at all, forget to argue with God, but those who would succeed, state their reasons and their strong arguments, and they debate the question with the Lord. Those who half-heartedly wrestle, randomly snatch at small things here and there, but those who are really wrestling have a certain way of grabbing hold of the opponent—a method of struggling with the request according to order and rule. The art of wrestling in faith is to plead with God, and say with holy boldness, "Let it be like this and this, for these reasons."

Hosea tells us about Jacob at Jabbok, where we can learn from him as an example. Now, the two pleas which Jacob used were God's command and God's promise. First, he said, *"O Lord who said to me, 'Return to your country and to your kindred"* (Gen 32:9), which would be the same as saying —"Lord, I am in difficulty, but I have come here in obedience to You. You told me to do this. Now, since You commanded me to come here, into the hands of my brother Esau, who comes to meet me like a lion, Lord, You cannot be so unfaithful to bring me into danger and then leave me in it."

This was a clear, strong argument, and it won God over. Then Jacob also added in a promise, *"But you said, 'I will surely do you good'"* (Gen 32:12). Among people, it is a very clever way of reasoning when you can challenge your opponent with his own words. You can quote other experts, and the person might say, "I don't recognize their authority," but, when you quote their own words against those people, you completely defeat them. When you remind a person about a promise they made, they either have to admit that they are unfaithful and inconsistent, or, if they acknowledge that they made the promise, and are true to their word, you have caught them, and won.

Let us learn how to plead the commands, the promises, and whatever else can benefit us, but let us always have something to appeal to. Don't think that you have prayed unless you have appealed, for pleading is the very marrow of prayer. The person who pleads well knows the secret of succeeding with God, especially if they plead the blood of Jesus because that unlocks the treasury of heaven. Many keys fit many locks, but the master key is the blood and the name of Jesus who died and rose again and lives forever in heaven to save to the very end.

There are many pleas in faith, and this is good, because faith is put in many different circumstances, and needs all the types of appeals. Faith has many needs and sees that there are pleas to be made in every case. I won't go through every single one of faith's different pleas, but I will mention a few, enough for us to see how many there are. Faith will plead all the characteristics of God. "You are just, so then spare the soul for whom the Savior died. You are merciful, so wipe away my transgressions. You are good, so reveal Your rewards to Your servant. You never change—You have done this and that for others, so you can do this and that for me. You are faithful, so you cannot break Your promise, or turn away from Your covenant." If we look at it properly, all the godly qualities become pleas for faith.

Faith will boldly plead all God's gracious relationships. It will say to Him, "Are You not the Creator? Will You forsake the works of Your own hands? Are You not the Redeemer? You have redeemed Your servant, will You cast me away?" Faith loves to take hold of the fatherhood of God. This is one of its master moves, and when it brings this one up, faith usually wins. "You are a Father, and would you discipline us as though You were going to kill us? You are a Father, and will You not provide? You are a Father, and have You got no sympathy and no compassion? You are a Father, and can You deny what Your own child asks of You?"

Whenever I am impressed with God's majesty, and sometimes a little discouraged in prayer, I find the quickest and the best cure is to remember that although He is a great King, and infinitely glorious, I am His child, and no matter who the father is, the child can always be bold with his father. Yes, faith can plead all of the relationships God has with His children.

Faith can also appeal with godly promises. I should not have to explain this too much, because I am sure most of us do this anyway. When you can bring God's own Word before Him, it is good. That is the conquering argument, "Do as you have said." "You have spoken it, and you have made your promise to be yes and amen in Jesus to your own glory, won't you fulfill it? Will you turn away from your own Word? Will you fail to carry out your own statements? That would not be like you, Lord!"

We want to be more businesslike and have common sense when we are pleading promises with. If you went to a bank and saw a man go in and produce a piece of paper, put it down on the counter, then retrieve it and do nothing else; if he did that several times a day, I think there would soon be orders to keep the man out, because he was just wasting the teller's time, and doing nothing purposeful.

Those businessmen who go to the bank and present their checks, wait until they receive their money and then they go, but not without having transacted real business. They do not put the paper down, speak about the excellent signature and discuss how correct the document is, but they want their money for it, and they are not content to leave without it. These are the people who are always welcome at the bank and not the time-wasters.

Unfortunately, many people play at praying, it is no better than a time-waster. When I say they play at praying, I mean that they do not expect God to give them an answer, and so they are just procrastinators who mock the Lord. The person who prays in a businesslike way, meaning what they say, honors the Lord. The Lord does not play at promising, Jesus did not pretend to confirm the Word by His blood, and we must not make a joke of prayer by going about it in a lazy, unexpecting manner.

The Holy Spirit is sincere, and we must be sincere too. We must aim for a blessing, and not be satisfied until we have it, like the hunter, who is not satisfied because he has run so many miles, and is never content until he catches his prey.

Faith also pleads the performances of God. It looks back on the past and says, "Lord, You delivered me on that occasion, will You fail me now?" Faith takes its whole life and pleads like this—

"After so much mercy past,

Will You let me sink at last?

"Have You brought me so far that I may be put to shame at the end?"

FAITH KNOWS how to bring the ancient mercies of God, and make them arguments for present favors. There is not enough time to even look at a thousandth of faith's pleas.

Sometimes, faith's pleas are quite remarkable. As we see in this verse, it is against the proud rule of human nature to plead—"*I am poor and needy; hasten to me, O God!*" It's the same as another prayer of David, "*For your name's sake, O Lord, pardon my guilt, for it is great*" (Psalm 25:11). It's not normal for people to pray this way. Often we say, "Lord, have mercy on me, for I am not as bad a sinner as some." But faith sees everything in a true light and bases its pleas on truth. "Lord, because my sin is great, and You are a great God, let Your great mercy be magnified in me."

We know the story of the Syrophenician woman; a wonderful example of the ingenuity of faith's reasoning. She came to Jesus about her daughter, and He did not even answer her. What do you think her heart said? Why, she said to herself, "It is good, for He has not denied me since He has not spoken at all, He has not refused me." With this as encouragement, she began to plead again. Then Jesus spoke to her with sharp words, and her brave heart said, "At last, He has said something to me, Soon I will also see Him act on my behalf."

That also encouraged her, and then, when He called her a dog, she reasoned that "a dog is a part of the family, it has some connection with the master of the house. Even though it doesn't eat meat from the table, it still gets the crumbs under it. So, even if I am a dog, You are the great Master, and the blessing that I ask of You, as big as it is for me, is only a crumb to You. Give it to me, I beg You." Could she fail to have her request met? Impossible! When faith has a will, it always finds a way, and it will win the day even when everything else spells defeat.

Faith's pleas are remarkable, but I must add, faith's pleas are always solid because it is a very revealing plea to admit that we are poor and needy. Isn't that the main argument with mercy? Necessity is the best plea with compassion, either human or divine. Isn't our need the best reason we can use? If we wanted a doctor to come quickly to a sick man, we would say, "It's not something common, he is about to die, come to him, come quickly!"

If we wanted the firefighters to rush to a fire, we wouldn't say to them, "Quickly, come, it is only a small fire." We would persuade them that it is an old house, full of combustible materials, and there are rumors of petrol and gunpowder on the premises. Also, it is near a timber yard, with many wooden cottages close by, and soon half the city could be up in flames." We paint the worst picture we can and state it as urgently as possible. We need the wisdom to be wise in pleading with God, to find arguments everywhere, but especially to find them in our needs.

Long ago that job of begging was the easiest one to do, but it paid the worst. It may have changed a bit since then. The trade of begging with God is still a hard one, but undoubtedly it pays the best of anything in the world. Interestingly, beggars on the streets often have many requests for different things. When someone is kicked out and is starving, they can usually find a reason to ask for aid from every likely person. Suppose it's a person to whom he already has a connection, then the poor tramp argues, "I can safely ask of him again, for he knows me, and has always been very kind." If they never asked from that person before, then they say, "I have never worried him before, he cannot say he has already done all he can for me, I will be bold and start asking him."

If it's one of the beggar's own family, then they will say, "Surely you will help me in my trouble, because we are relatives." If it's a stranger, they will say, "I have often found strangers kinder than my own family, help me, I beg you." If they ask from the rich, they plead that they will never miss what they give, and if they beg from the poor, they also know what it is to be in need, and will find sympathy from him in their time of trouble.

I wish we were half as alert in filling our mouths with arguments when we are before the Lord. How is it that we are half asleep, and don't seem to have our spiritual senses awakened? May God help us to learn the art of pleading with Him, because there we will succeed, through the merit of Jesus Christ.

An Urgent Heart

We will quickly look at the last point; an urgent soul. *"Hasten to me, O God!...do not delay!"*

We might be urgent with God if we are not born again, because our need is critical; we are in terrible danger, and it is the worst kind of danger. In the next hour, in the next minute, if you are a sinner, you might be in a place where there is no more hope. So, cry out, *"hasten to me, O God! You are my help and my deliverer; O Lord, do not delay!"* You can't afford to wait if this is you; you don't have time to procrastinate, therefore, be urgent, because your need is urgent. And remember, if you really are in need, and the Spirit of God is at work in you, you must be urgent.

An ordinary sinner might be happy to wait, but a sinner that has been awakened wants mercy now. A dead sinner will lie quiet, but a living sinner can't rest until forgiveness is sealed in his heart. If you are desperate today, I am happy about that, because your urgency comes from the possession of spiritual life. When you can't live without a Savior any longer, the Savior will come to you, and you will rejoice in Him.

As I have said on another point, the same truth is good to hold onto. God will come to bless you, and come quickly when your sense of need becomes deep and urgent. Oh, how great is the church's need! We will grow cold, unholy, and worldly, there will be no conversions, there will be no new people coming in, there will be people leaving, there will be divisions, there will be all kinds of problems. Satan will rejoice, and Jesus will be dishonored unless we receive a larger measure of the Holy Spirit. Our need is urgent, and when we really feel that need, then we will get the blessing that we want.

Does a melancholic spirit say, "We are in such a bad state that we can't expect a large blessing"? My answer would be that if we were in a worse state, we might receive it even sooner. I don't mean if we were really like that, but if we felt we were worse, we should be closer to the blessing. When we mourn over the terrible state we are in, then we cry the more forcefully to God, the blessing comes. God never refused to go with Gideon because he didn't have enough brave men with him, but He waited because there were too many people. He brought the numbers of soldiers down from thousands to hundreds, and He sent away the hundreds before He gave them victory. When you feel that you must find God's presence, but that you don't deserve it, and when this brings you to your knees, then the blessing will be given.

For me, I desire to feel a spirit of urgency in my heart as I plead with God for the dew of His grace to descend on the church. I am not shy about this, because I have a license to pray. Begging might be forbidden in the streets, but, before the Lord, I am a licensed beggar. Jesus has said that we *"ought always to pray and not lose heart"* (Luke 18:1).

You land on the shores of a foreign country with the greatest confidence when you carry a passport with you, and God has issued passports to His children. With these, we can come boldly to His mercy seat, He has invited us, He has encouraged us, He has commanded us to come to Him, and He has promised that whatever we ask in prayer, believing, we will receive. So, come—come urgently, come persistently, come with this plea, *"I am poor and needy; hasten to me, O God!"* and a blessing will definitely come, it will not wait long. God let us see it, and give Him the glory of it.

A Heart that Holds onto God

We may have rushed a bit over the last point, where I could have expounded more, but we must look at the fourth point. Here is another part of the art and mystery of prayer—the soul-grasping God.

We have pleaded, and we have been urgent, but now we come very close and take hold of the Angel of the Lord. With one hand we hold on and say, "You are my help," and with the other, "You are my deliverer." What incredible 'my's,' those powerful 'my's.' The wonder of the Bible is in the possessive pronouns, and if we are taught to use them as the psalmist did, we will become conquerors with the eternal

God. Now, sinner, I pray that God has helped you to say to Jesus, *"You are my help and my deliverer"* (Psalm 40:17).

Maybe you are sorry that you can't reach far enough, but have you got no other help? You cannot hold two helpers with the same hand. "Oh, no," you say, "I have no help anywhere. I have no hope except in Christ." Well, since your hand is empty, that empty hand was made to grab onto your Lord and hold onto Him! Say to Him, "Lord, I will hang onto You as Jacob did, now I can't help myself, I will cling to You, I will not let You go until You bless me."

"That is being too bold," someone might say. But the Lord loves boldness in poor sinners, He would rather you were more courageous and bold than you think you are. It's a wicked shyness that doesn't trust a crucified Savior. He died on purpose to save us as we are, let Him have His way with you, and trust Him.

"Oh," someone else says, "but I am so unworthy." Jesus came to seek and save the unworthy. He is not the Savior of the self-righteous, He is the sinners' Savior—"friend of sinners" is His name. Unworthy person, take hold of Him!

"Oh," another person says, "but I have no right." That is the very reason you should reach out for Him because right is for the court of justice, not for the hall of mercy. I would advise you not to try your rights, because you have no right but to be condemned, but you need no rights when dealing with Jesus. A generous person will not give money to a beggar who says, "I have a right." Then the person would answer, "If you have rights, go and get them, I will give you nothing." Since you have no right, your need becomes your claim, it is all the claim you want. Someone might add, "It's too late for me to plead for grace." That is impossible. While you live and desire mercy, it is never too late to seek it.

Take a look at the parable of the man who wanted three loaves of bread. When I read it, I thought about why the man went to his friend so late, at midnight. His friend would have said to him that it was too late, but still, the man received the bread he asked for. In the parable, he could not have gone any later, because if it had been after midnight, it would have been early the next morning, and so would not have been late, but early. If it is midnight with your heart, don't give up, Jesus is an out-of-season Savior, many of His servants are *"untimely born"* (1 Cor 15:8). He doesn't work according to our seasons and times.

Any season is the right season to call on the name of Jesus; so, don't let the devil tempt you with the thought that it is too late. Go to Jesus now, and grab hold of the horns of the altar by a daring faith, and say, "Sacrifice for sinners, You are a sacrifice for me. Intercessor for the graceless, you are an intercessor for me. You who give gifts to the rebellious, give gifts to me, for I have been a rebel. When we were without strength, Christ died for the ungodly. That's what I am, Jesus, let the power of Your death be seen in me to save my soul."

Those of you that are saved and love Christ, I want you, as Christians, to practice this last point I am making, and make sure you take hold of God in prayer. *"You are my help and my deliverer."* As a church we must throw ourselves on the strength of God because we can do nothing without Him; we don't want to be without Him, we will hold Him tightly. *"You are my help and my deliverer."*

According to an old story, there was a boy in Athens who used to boast that he ruled all of Athens. When they asked him how this was possible he said, "Well, I rule my mother, my mother rules my father, and my father rules the city." The person that knows how to be a master in prayer will rule the heart of Jesus, and Jesus can and will do all things for His people because the Father has given everything into His hands.

You can be powerful too, if you know how to pray, omnipotent in all things which glorify God. What does the Bible say? *"Let them lay hold of my protection"* (Isaiah 27:5). Prayer moves the hand that moves the world. How we need the grace to grab hold of Almighty love in this way. We want more adhesive prayer, more tugging, and gripping, and wrestling prayer, that says, "I will not let You go."

That picture of Jacob at Jabbok is enough for us to finish on. The Angel of the Lord is there, and Jacob wants a blessing from Him. The angel seems to try and put him off, but no put-offs will do for Jacob. Then the angel tries to escape from him, and pulls and makes every effort to get free, but nothing will make Jacob relax his grasp. At last, the angel turns from ordinary wrestling to wounding him where it weakens Jacob. But, Jacob will let his hip go, and all his arms and legs go, but he will not let the angel go.

The poor man's strength disappears under the touch, but in his weakness, he is still strong. He throws his arms about the mysterious man and holds Him as if in a death grip. Then the angel says, *"Let me go, for the day has broken"* (Gen 32:26). Notice that He did not shake Jacob off; He only said, "Let me go." The angel won't do anything to force him to relax his hold, He leaves that up to his voluntary will. The triumphant Jacob cries, "No, I won't give up, I am determined to win an answer to my prayer. *I will not let you go unless you bless me"* (Gen 32:26).

Now, when the church begins to pray, at first, the Lord will push us as if He wants us to go further, and we might be worried that no answer will be given. Hold on, Christians. Be steadfast, unmovable, in spite of everything. As you hold on, discouragement will come instead of the success we hoped for, fellow Christians will try to stop us or dissuade us, some will be lazy, and others sinning, backsliders and unrepentant people will come near, but we must not be turned away from our goal. We must become even more eager. And if we do become discouraged and depressed, and feel that we have never been as weak as we are now, don't worry, still hold on, for when the muscles are weak, the victory is near. Hold on with a tighter grasp than before. Let this be our resolution, *"I will not let you go unless you bless me."*

Remember, the longer it takes for the blessing to come, the richer it will be when it arrives. That which is gained quickly by a single prayer is sometimes only a second-rate blessing, but that which is gained after many desperate tugs and pulls, and many awful struggles, is a full and precious blessing. Persistent Christians are always beautiful to look at. The blessing that costs us the most prayer will be worth the most. May we be persevering in prayer, so we can receive a larger blessing for ourselves, the church, and the world. I wish it were in my power to stir you all up into passionate prayer, but I must leave that for the great author of all true supplication—the Holy Spirit. May He work in us mightily, for Jesus' sake. Amen.

(A sermon on October 29, 1871, at the Metropolitan Tabernacle, Newington).

Study Guide

Having your Bible close by as you read is a really good way to immerse yourself in what is being spoken about. It gives context and shows the credibility of what Spurgeon is saying. Also, as Christians, we know that God speaks through His Word. If you remember or know of verses that relate to the topic or the questions being discussed, look them up, write them down, and make a study of them. This will deepen your knowledge and understanding of what is being shared.

Spurgeon's sermon is all about the heart. Our relationship with Jesus is all about the heart. To have the right heart when we come to prayer is very important.

1. Besides the examples from the Bible that are given, are there any 'masters' of prayer in your life that you can learn from?
2. When the word confession is used, we often think of admitting all of our sins, but Spurgeon is not just talking about that here. What does he mean by a confessing heart?
3. Pleading makes us think of simply begging, but again, we need to understand the full meaning of the

word as it is used here. What do you understand by a pleading heart?
4. Can you give some other words for 'urgent' as it is used here? Do you have an urgent heart?
5. We often hear stories of people who pray for one thing for years; never giving up. Do you fit into that category?
6. The Bible talks a lot about waiting. It seems like one of the hardest things for us as humans to do. Read these verses and discuss them:

Romans 12:12, Psalm 27:14, 2 Peter 3:9, Exodus 14:14, Isaiah 30:18, 2 Peter 3:8

5

THE THRONE OF GRACE

"The throne of grace."
Hebrews 4:16

These words are found in that wonderful verse, *"Let us then with confidence draw near to the throne of grace, that we may receive mercy and find grace to help in time of need"* (Heb 4:16). They are a gem in a golden setting. True prayer is the heart led by the Spirit to approach the throne of God. It is not the words that are spoken, it is not just the feeling of desires, but it is the advance of the desires to God, the spiritual approach of our nature towards the Lord our God.

True prayer isn't a simple mental exercise, nor a vocal performance; it is far deeper than that—it is a spiritual exchange with the Creator of heaven and earth. God is a Spirit that our human eyes cannot see, and He can only be perceived by our spirit within us. Renewed by the Holy Spirit when we were born again, our spirit discerns God, communicates with Him, brings our requests to Him, and receives answers of peace from Him. It's a spiritual business from start to finish. Its aim and objective don't end with man but reach to God Himself.

In order to pray this way, the work of the Holy Spirit is needed. If prayer was only dependent on our mouths, we would just need breath in our nostrils to pray. Prayer is also not only about desires. Many good desires are easily felt, even by non-Christians. But when it is a spiritual desire, and the spiritual fellowship of our spirit with God, then the Holy Spirit must be there, to help infirmity, and give life and power, or else true prayer will never happen. Without this, whatever is offered to God will have the name and the form of prayer, but the inner life of prayer will not be there.

If we look at our verse, we can clearly see that Jesus is also essential to acceptable prayer. Just as prayer cannot be real prayer without the Spirit of God, so it will not be successful prayer without the Son of God. As the Great High Priest, Jesus can go past the veil for us, but through His crucifixion, the veil can be completely removed. Until then, we are shut out from the living God. Anyone who, despite what the Bible says, tries to pray without a Savior insults God. They make a big mistake imagining that their own natural desires, coming up before God without the precious blood, will be an acceptable sacrifice before God. They have not brought an offering that God can accept, instead, they have offered an unclean sacrifice. Worked in us by the Spirit, presented for us by

Jesus, prayer becomes powerful before the Most High. That is the only way!

To try and stir your hearts that they might be led to come near to the throne of grace, I want to look at this verse with God's help.

You have begun to pray. God has begun to answer. In the church, more people have come forward to confess Christ—a clear answer to the requests of God's people, as though His hand had stretched down from heaven and handed us the blessings we asked for. Now, let us continue in prayer. Let us become stronger in intercession, and the more we succeed, the more sincere we will be to succeed even more. Let us not be poor in our hearts, because we are not poor in our God. This is a good day and a time of encouragement. Since we have the King's ear, I am eager for us to speak to Him for thousands of others, that they might also come to Jesus through our prayers.

In trying to explore the verse, I want to look at it in these parts: First, we have a throne. Secondly, there is grace. Then we will put them together, and we shall see grace on a throne, and finally, putting all of those together in another order, we will see sovereignty shining in grace.

A Throne

The first part of our verse to look at is the throne: "The throne of grace."

In prayer, God is seen as our Father. That is the view we find the easiest and most precious to us. But even then, we must not see Him as an earthly father, because Jesus told us that He is *"Our Father in heaven"* (Matt 6:9). And to remind us that our Father is much greater than ourselves, He teaches us to say, *"Hallowed be your name. Your kingdom come"* (Matt 6:9-10). In this way, God our Father is also seen as a King. When we pray, we are not just coming before our Father's feet, but we come also to the throne of the King of the universe. The mercy seat is a throne, and we must not forget this.

If we view prayer as an entrance into the royal courts of heaven and realize we need to behave as court attendants in the presence of great majesty, then we will know the right spirit in which to pray. If in prayer, we come to a throne, it is clear that our spirit should be one of humble reverence. It is expected that when a subject is approaching the king, they should show respect and honor. Any pride that will not bow to the king, or any treason that rebels against the sovereign would be wise enough to avoid coming near to the throne.

Pride needs to be dealt with out in the streets. Treason must hide in the corner because only humble reverence can come before the king when he sits in his robes of majesty. In our case, the King that we come to is the greatest of all, the King of kings, and the Lord of lords. Emperors are just shadows of His imperial power. They call themselves kings by the right of royalty, but what right do they have? Common sense laughs at their claims of royalty.

Only the Lord alone has the divine right, and the kingdom belongs to Him, no one else. He is the blessed and only ruler. All the rest are just nominal kings, that are set up, and put down at the will of men, or the decree of providence, but He is Lord alone, the Prince of the kings of the earth.

"He sits on no precarious throne, Nor borrows leave to be."

My heart, make sure you bow down in such a presence. If He is so great, put your mouth in the dust before Him, for He is the most powerful of all kings. His throne has influence in all worlds. Heaven obeys Him, Hell trembles before Him, and earth is forced to surrender willingly or unwillingly. His power can make or can destroy. To create or to crush is easy for Him. My heart, make sure that when you come near to the Omnipotent, the consuming fire, you take off your shoes, and worship Him with humility.

He is also the most holy of all kings. His throne is the great white throne, as clean and clear as crystal. *"God puts no trust in his holy ones, and the heavens are not pure in his sight"* (Job 15:15). So, for us sinners, how low and humble should we be when we come to Him? We may know Him, but let it be with respect and reverence. We may be bold, but let it be without pride or arrogance. We are on earth and He is in heaven. We are like worms of ground, creatures crushed before the moth; He is the Everlasting. Before the mountains were made, He was God, and if all created things should pass away again, He will still remain the same.

I am worried that we don't bow before the Eternal Majesty as we should. From this moment, let us ask the Spirit to give us the right attitude, that every one of our prayers may approach the Infinite Majesty in reverence.

Not only with respect and reverence, but secondly, we should also approach with joy. If I realize that I have favor through grace to stand with all of those who are in His courts, would I not feel glad? I might have been in His prison, but now I am before His throne. I might have been expelled from His presence forever, but now I am allowed to come near to Him, even into His royal palace, into His throne room. Shouldn't I be thankful? Shouldn't my thankfulness rise up into joy, and should I not feel honored to be able to receive blessing and favor when I pray?

Why are you sad when you stand before the throne of grace? If you were before the throne of justice to be condemned for your sins, your hands might hang low in despair, but now you are favored to come before the King in His love, let your face shine with holy joy. If your sorrows are heavy, tell Him about them, because He can relieve them. If your sins are many, confess them, because He can forgive them. Those of you that come into the halls of this King, be incredibly glad and mix praises in with your prayers.

Thirdly, whenever we come before a throne, it should be in complete submission. We don't pray to God to tell Him what He must do, nor should we presume to dictate His will to Him. We are permitted to say to God, "This and that if we can have it," but we should also add, "But since we are ignorant and could be mistaken—seeing that we are still in the flesh, and might be driven by carnal motives—not our will, but Your will."

Who can dictate to the throne? No loyal Christian could imagine taking the place of the King. Instead, we bow before

Him, because He has the right to be Lord of all, and even though we pray sincerely, passionately, persistently, and we plead and plead again, it should always be with a submissive attitude: "Your will be done, my Lord, and if I ask anything that is not in line with that, would You be good enough to deny me. I will accept Your answer if You refuse me for asking for something that is not good in Your sight."

If we can remember this, I think we wouldn't push certain requests before the throne, because we would feel, "I am here looking for my own way, my own comfort, and my own advantage. Maybe I am asking for something that will dishonor God, so I will speak with the deepest submission."

In the fourth place, if it is a throne, it should be approached with great expectations. The old hymn puts it like this:

"You are coming to a King:

Large petitions with you bring."

We do not just come in prayer to God's storehouse where He gives out His blessings to the poor, nor do we come to the back door to receive the broken scraps, though that is more than we deserve. To eat the crumbs that fall from the Master's table is more than we could claim. But when we pray, we are standing in the palace, on the glittering floor of the great King's own reception room, and so, we have an advantage. In prayer, we stand where angels bow down, and the cherubim and seraphim adore Him. It is the same throne that our prayers go up to. Should we come there with half-hearted requests and limited and reduced faith?

No, it is not like a king to give away pennies and cents, He distributes pieces of gold. He doesn't throw out scraps of bread and leftover meat like we do, but He holds a feast of rich food, of fat meat full of marrow and refined wine.

When Alexander the Great's soldier was told to ask for whatever he wanted, he didn't ask for something small according to what he deserved, but he made such a heavy demand that the royal treasurer refused to pay it. The case was brought to Alexander, and Alexander as a king, replied, "He knows how great Alexander is, and he has asked as from a king. Let him have what he requests."

We must be careful not to imagine that God's thoughts are like our thoughts, and His ways are our ways. We mustn't bring feeble requests and petty needs before God, saying, "Lord, can You do these?" We must remember that as high as the heavens are above the earth, so are His ways above our ways and His thoughts above our thoughts. Therefore, we should ask God for great things, for we are before a great throne. If we always felt this way when we came before the throne of grace, then He would do for us exceeding abundantly above what we ask or even think.

Let me add a fifth way to come before the throne of grace. We should approach with steady faith. Who can doubt the King? Who dares challenge the imperial word? If integrity was banished from the hearts of all mankind, it would still live in the hearts of kings. Shame on a king if he can lie. The poorest beggar in the streets is dishonored by a broken promise, but what can we say about a king if his word cannot be depended upon?

Shame on us if we are unbelieving before the throne of the King of heaven and earth. With our God before us in all His glory, sitting on the throne of grace, will we say that we don't trust Him? Can we imagine that He cannot, or will not, keep His promise? Such blasphemous thoughts must be banished. However, if they do come, let it be when we are somewhere outside of His kingdom if there is such a place, and not in prayer, when we are in His presence and glory of His throne of grace. That is the place for the child to trust its Father, for the loyal subject to trust his king, far from any doubt or suspicion. Unshakeable faith should be in us when we come before the mercy seat.

There is only one more point, and that is, if prayer is coming before the throne of God, it should always be with the deepest sincerity, and in a spirit that makes everything real. If you are disloyal enough to despise the King, then don't mock Him to His face. When He is on His throne, if you dare repeat holy words anywhere without your heart being in it, let it not be in Jehovah's palace.

If a person asks for an audience with royalty, and then says, "I hardly know why I have come. I don't know if I have anything specific to ask. I have no very urgent business to address," they would be guilty of being foolish and dishonorable? As for our great King, when we come into His presence, let us have a real reason to be there.

As I said before, let us watch out that we don't play at praying. It is an insult to God. If I am called on to pray in public, I mustn't use words that please the ears of those around me, but I must realize that I am speaking to God Himself and that I have a business to attend to with the Lord. And in my private prayer, when I get up in the morning, and I bow my knees and repeat certain words, or when I go to bed at night and go through the same regular form, I am actually sinning rather than doing anything good, unless my heart is speaking to the Most High.

Do you think that the King of heaven is delighted to hear you pronounce words with a flippant tongue and a thoughtless mind? Then You don't know Him. He is a Spirit, and those who worship Him must do so in spirit and in truth. If you have any empty lists to read out, go and tell them to fools that will listen but not before the Lord of hosts.

If you have certain words that you try to make and make sound important, go and say them in the loud, brash 'Roman' courts, but not before the Lord of Zion. The spiritual God seeks spiritual worshippers, and He will only accept those who are. The sacrifice of the wicked is an abomination to the Lord, and only a sincere prayer is His delight.

If I had to sum up all the points so far, it's this—prayer is not an insignificant matter. It's an important and superior act. It is a wonderful privilege. Under the Old Persian Empire, a few of the nobility were permitted to come to the king whenever they wanted, and this was thought to be the highest privilege for normal people.

You and I, as Christians, have a permit, a passport to come before the throne of heaven at any time we want, and we are encouraged to go in with great boldness. But let us not forget that it's not a small thing to be an attendant in the courts of heaven and earth, to worship Him who made us, and sustains us. When we try and pray, we might hear that glorious voice saying, "Bow the knee." All the angels that see the face of our Father in heaven, call us to *"Oh come, let us worship and bow down; let us kneel before the Lord, our Maker! For he is our God, and we are the people of his pasture and the sheep of his hand...Worship the Lord in the splendor of holiness; tremble before him, all the earth!"* (Psalm 95:6, 96:9).

Grace

If the glow and brilliance of the word 'throne' are too much for us, our verse now shows us the soft, gentle radiance of that delightful word, 'grace.'

We are called to the throne of grace, not to the throne of law. Sinai was once the throne of law when God came to Paran with ten thousand of His people. Who wanted to come near to that throne? Not even Israel wanted to. Boundaries were set about the mountain, and if an animal touched the mountain, it was stoned or stabbed to death. Those who are self-righteous, who think they can obey the law, and think that they can be saved by it, look at the fire that Moses saw, and shrink back, tremble, and despair.

We don't come to that throne now, because through Jesus it has changed. To a mind that is cleansed by the precious blood, there is no anger on the holy throne. But without that blood, our troubled minds see—

"Once it was a seat of burning wrath,

And shot devouring flames.

Our God appeared a consuming fire,

And jealous was His name."

AND THANK GOD, we are not speaking about the throne of justice. We will all come before that one day, and those who have believed will find it to be a throne of grace as well as of justice because He who sits on that throne will not pass a sentence of condemnation against anyone who is justified by faith.

But we are not looking at the place where the resurrection trumpet will play its final notes. We will not talk about the angels with their vengeful swords coming to destroy the enemies of God. It's not time to see the gates of hell open up to swallow those who did not want the Son of God to reign over them. We are still on praying ground, and pleading with God, and the throne that we come to, and of which we now speak, is the throne of grace.

It is a throne set up to impart grace. A throne from which every word spoken is of grace. The scepter that stretches out from it is the silver scepter of grace. The commands proclaimed from it are purposes of grace. The blessings that are scattered down its golden steps are gifts of grace, and He who sits on the throne is grace itself. It's the throne of grace that we come to when we pray, and let us think about this for a bit, as an extra encouragement for those who are learning to pray. And for all of us who are praying men and women.

If in prayer, I come before the throne of grace, then the faults of my prayers will be overlooked. When you are just starting to pray you feel as if you are not really praying. The groans of your spirit, when you get up off your knees, are ones that you think very little of. What a chaotic, unfocused, broken prayer it is. Don't worry, you haven't come to the throne of justice, otherwise, God would have rejected it when He saw the mistakes and errors. Your broken words, your gasps, and stammering are before a throne of grace.

When any of us has presented his best prayer before God, if we saw it the way God sees it, there is no doubt we would cry over it, for there is enough sin in the best prayer ever prayed to make sure it is turned down by God. But, I repeat, it's not a throne of justice, and this is the hope for our weak, shambles of a prayer. Our King doesn't keep up a stately etiquette in His court like those we find in earthly palaces, where a little mistake or an error would see the petitioners dismissed with disgrace.

The faulty cries of His children are not severely criticized by Him. Jesus, the Lord of the palace above, takes time to fix and change every prayer before He presents it. He makes the prayer perfect with His perfection, and successful with His own merits. God looks on the prayer, as it is presented through Christ, and forgives all its defects. This should encourage any of us who feel weak, unsure, and unskilled in prayer. If you can't plead with God as you did years ago if you feel as if you have become rusty in this area, never give up, but keep coming to the throne, because it is not one of severe criticism, it's a throne of grace we come to.

And because it is a throne of grace, the faults of the person praying will not prevent the success of the prayer being offered. There are so many faults in all of us! We are not fit and worthy to come before the throne of God. We are all polluted with sin inside and out! How can any of us think of praying if God's throne was not a throne of grace? Maybe you can, but I certainly can't.

An absolute God, holy and just, could not in keeping with His divine nature answer any prayer from a sinner like me unless He has made a plan where my prayer no longer comes up to a throne of absolute justice, but to a throne that is also the mercy seat. It is the appeasement, the place where God meets sinners, through Jesus Christ. I couldn't tell you to pray unless it was before a throne of grace; I couldn't even talk about prayer to you sinners.

But now I will say this to every sinner, even though you might think you are the worst sinner that ever lived; cry to the Lord and seek Him while He may be found. A throne of grace is a place made for you. Get on your knees. By simple faith, go to your Savior, because it is He who is the throne of grace. It is in Him that God is able to show grace to the guiltiest person. Thank God, neither the faults of the prayer nor the sin of the person praying will keep our requests from God who delights in broken and contrite hearts.

If it's a throne of grace, then the desires of the one praying will be understood. If I can't find the words to speak my wants and needs, God in His grace will know them without the words. He takes the meaning of us Christians, the meaning of our groans. A throne that was not gracious would not waste time trying to understand our petitions, but God is gracious, and will dive into the heart of our desires, and will read what we cannot say with our mouths.

Have you ever seen a parent, when the child is trying to say something, and they know exactly what the little one is trying to say, helps him over the words, and even speaks the syllables for him? And if the little one has forgotten what he wants to say, you will see the father suggest the word. It's the same with the Spirit, from the throne of grace, He will help us and teach us words, He will write our desires in our hearts.

In the Bible, there are stories of God putting words into sinners' mouths. He tells us *"Take with you words and return to the Lord; say to him, 'Take away all iniquity; accept what is good'"* (Hos 14:2). He will put the desires and the expression of those desires into our spirit by His grace. He will direct our desires to the things which we should be seeking for. He will teach us what we need and want, even though we don't know them yet. He will suggest His promises to us so that we can plead them. He will be the Alpha and Omega to our prayers, just as He is to our salvation, because in the same way salvation is of grace from beginning to end, so the sinner's approach to the throne of grace is of grace from first to last.

What encouragement! Won't we come near to this throne with greater boldness as we realize the true meaning of this precious phrase, "The throne of grace"?

If it's a throne of grace, then all the needs of those who come to it will be supplied. The King that sits on such a throne will not say, "You must bring Me gifts. You must offer Me sacrifices." It's not a throne for receiving tributes. It's a throne for giving out gifts. Come then, those who are as poor as poverty itself. Come, those of you who have no merits, and are lacking in character and morals. Come, all of you who are bankrupt because of Adam's fall and by your own sins. This is not the throne of majesty which supports itself by taxing its subjects, but a throne that glorifies itself by a flood of good things. Come now, and receive the wine and milk that are freely given; come buy wine and milk without money, and without price. All the needs of those who ask will be supplied because it is a throne of grace.

Added to this, even the petitioner's sorrows will be comforted. Imagine that I come to the throne of grace with my burden of sins. There is One on the throne who felt the burden of sin long ago and has not forgotten what it's like. What if I come heavy with sorrow? There is One who knows all the sorrows that people have to face. Am I depressed and discouraged? Do I worry that God has forsaken me? There is One on the throne who said, *"My God, my God, why have you forsaken me?"* (Matt 27:46).

It's a throne from which grace loves to look at our troubles and anxieties, tenderly consider them, and relieve them. Come, then. Come, then. Come then, you who are not only poor but wretched. If your troubles make you long for death, but you fear it. If you are captive, come in your chains. If you are a slave, come with the chains on your hearts. If you sit in darkness, come with your blindfold still on. The throne of grace will look on you if you can't look on it, and will give to you, even though you have nothing to give in return, and will deliver you, even though you can't lift a finger to deliver yourself.

"The throne of grace." The phrase grows as I think about it more and more in my mind, and to me, it is an incredible thought that if I come to the throne of God in prayer, I might feel a thousand defects, but there is still hope. I usually feel more dissatisfied with my prayers than with anything else I do. I don't believe that it's an easy thing to pray in public to properly lead a large congregation. We sometimes hear a person being commended for preaching well, but if anyone can learn to pray well, there will be an equal gift and a higher grace in it.

But what if we lack knowledge in prayer? It's a throne of grace, and our Father knows that we need these things. What if we lack faith? He sees our little faith and still does not reject it, as small as it is. He does not measure out His gifts by the degree of our faith, but by the sincerity and reality of faith. And if anything is lacking in our spirit, and something wrong with our passion, or in the humility of the prayer, still grace overlooks all this, forgives all this, and its merciful hand is stretched out to enrich us according to our needs. Surely, this should encourage many people to pray who have not prayed and should make us who are already accustomed to it, to use the art of prayer, to draw near with greater boldness than before to the throne of grace.

Grace Enthroned

If we look at the whole verse, it conveys to us the idea of grace enthroned.

It's a throne but who sits on it? It's grace personified sitting there in dignity—grace is on the throne. In the Gospel of Jesus Christ, grace is the most predominant attribute of God. Why is it so exalted? It's because grace has a throne by conquest. Grace came down to earth in the form of Jesus and met with sin. The struggle was long and difficult, and it looked as though grace was going to be squashed and defeated by sin. But grace finally took hold of sin, lifted it onto its own shoulders, and even though the burden of it was heavy enough to crush, grace carried sin up to the cross, nailed it there, destroyed it, put it to death forever, and triumphed gloriously. For this reason, grace sits on a throne, because it has conquered sin, has taken the penalty of human guilt, and overthrown all its enemies.

Not just that, but grace sits on the throne because it has a right to be there. There is no injustice in the grace of God. God is as just when He forgives a believer, as when He casts a sinner into hell. I believe that in my heart there is also a justice that accepts the person who believes in Christ, and at the same time, rejects those who die without repenting, and are banished from God's presence.

The sacrifice of Jesus has enabled God to be just and justify those that believe. Anyone who knows the meaning of the word, 'substitution,' will see that Christians are free from having to pay their dues to justice because Jesus has paid all their debts. God would be unjust if He didn't save those for whom Christ suffered as a substitute, for whom His righteousness was provided, and to whom it is accredited. Grace is on the throne by conquest and sits there by right.

Grace is enthroned because Jesus has finished His work, and gone into the heavens. It is enthroned in power. When we speak of its throne, we mean that it has unlimited power. Grace doesn't sit at the footstool of God. Grace doesn't stand in the courts of God. It sits on the throne. It is the reigning attribute. It is the King today. This is the outpouring of grace, the time of grace. Grace reigns through righteousness to eternal life. We live in the time of reigning grace because He lives to make intercession for the sons of men, Jesus is also able to save those who come to Him by God, to the very end.

Sinner, if you were to meet grace on the road, like a traveler on his journey, I beg you to get to know it and ask for its influence. If you should meet grace as a financial businessman, with wealth in its hand , I beg you to become friends, because it will enrich you when you are in need. If you see grace as a friend of heaven, highly exalted, I beg you to call to it.

But when grace sits on the throne, I beg you to come close to it immediately. There is nothing higher or greater because God is love, which is another name for grace. Come and bow before it. Come and adore the infinite mercy and grace of God. Don't doubt, don't stop, don't hesitate. Grace is reigning. Grace is God. God is love.

If you can see that grace is enthroned, come and receive it. I have said that grace is enthroned by conquest, by right, and by power, and I will also add, it is enthroned in glory, for God glorifies His grace. It is one of His goals to make His grace honored. He loves to forgive those who repent, and in this way, show His forgiving grace. He loves to find those who wander off and restore them, to show His reclaiming grace. He loves to bring the broken-hearted and comfort them, that He may show His comforting grace.

There is grace available to us in so many forms, or rather the same grace acting in different ways, and God loves to make His grace glorious. There is a rainbow around the throne like an emerald, the emerald of His compassion and His love. How happy we are if we can believe this and come and glorify grace by becoming examples of its power at work in us.

The Glory of Grace

Lastly, if we read our verse correctly, we will see that it talks of sovereignty in glory—the glory of grace.

The mercy seat is a throne, and even though grace is there, it is still a throne. Grace does not take away the sovereignty. Now the characteristic of sovereignty is majestic and awesome—its light is like a jasper and a sapphire stone, most precious—as Ezekiel calls it, the *"awe-inspiring crystal"* (Ezek 1:22).

This is what the King, the Lord of hosts says: *"I will have mercy on whom I have mercy, and I will have compassion on whom I have compassion…But who are you, O man, to answer back to God? Will what is molded say to its molder, 'Why have you made me like this?' Has the potter no right over the clay, to make out of the same lump done vessel for honorable use and another for dishonorable use?"* (Rom 9:15,20-21).

These are harsh words that are not to be answered. He is a King, and He will do what He wants. No one can stop His hand or say to Him, "What are you doing?"

But before you become discouraged by the thought of His sovereignty, let's look back at the verse. It is a throne—there is sovereignty. But to every heart that knows how to pray, to every heart that comes to Jesus by faith, the true mercy seat, divine sovereignty is not something to be feared but is full of love. It is a throne of grace where the sovereignty of God to a Christian, to a pleader, to one who comes to God in Jesus, is always shown in pure grace.

To you who come to God in prayer, the sovereignty answers and says, "I will have mercy on that sinner, even though he doesn't deserve it, even though there is no merit in him, but because I can do what I want with My own, I will bless him. I will make him My child. I will accept him. He will be Mine in the day when I make up My jewels." On the mercy seat, God only carries out His sovereignty in grace. He reigns, but in this case, grace reigns through righteousness to eternal life by Jesus Christ our Lord.

To close off with, there are a few things to think about.

On the throne of grace, sovereignty has placed itself under a pledge of love. I will choose my words carefully and will make sure to say the right sentences because I don't want to say the wrong thing while trying to speak the truth clearly. God will do what He wants, but on the mercy seat, He is under an oath—one that He has made because He has entered into covenant with Jesus, and so He enters into covenant with His chosen people. Though God is and always must be a sovereign, He will never break His covenant, nor change the Word that has gone out of His mouth. He cannot be false to a covenant that He has made. When I come to God in Jesus, to God on the mercy seat, I don't need to imagine that through any act of sovereignty God will set aside His covenant. That cannot happen, it's impossible.

Added to this, on the throne of grace, God is again bound to us by His promises. The covenant contains in it many gracious promises that are great and precious. *"Ask, and it will be given to you; seek, and you will find; knock, and it will be opened to you"* (Matt 7:7). Until God had said those words or words similar to them, it was up to Him whether He wanted to hear prayer or not, but it is not that way now. For now, if it is true prayer offered through Jesus Christ, His truth binds Him to hear it.

A person can be perfectly free, but the moment they make a promise, they are not free to break it, and the everlasting God will not break His promise. He delights to fulfill it. He has declared that all His promises are yes and amen in Jesus. But for our comfort, when we see God as a sovereign, we must remember that He is bound by covenant promise to be faithful to those hearts that seek Him. His throne must be a throne of grace to His people.

And the sweetest thought of all is that every covenant promise has been endorsed and sealed with blood, and the last thing the everlasting God will do, is to disregard the blood of His dear Son. When a king issued a document outlining the rights of a city, before that he may have been absolute, and there may have been nothing to challenge his power and authority, but when the city has its charter, then it can plead its rights before the king.

In the same way, God has given to His people a charter of incredible blessing, granting them the mercies of David. Just as the authenticity of a charter depends on the signature and the seal, how guaranteed is the charter of covenant grace. The signature is God's, and the seal is the blood of Jesus. The covenant is confirmed with blood, the blood of His own dear Son.

It's not possible for us to plead in vain with God when we plead the blood-sealed covenant, clear and true. Heaven and earth will pass away, but the power of the blood of Jesus with God can never fail. It speaks when we are silent, and it succeeds when we are defeated. It asks for better things than Abel could ask for, and its cry is heard. Let us come boldly, for we have the promise in our hearts. When we feel afraid because of the sovereignty of God, let us sing joyfully,

"The Gospel bears my spirit up,

A faithful and unchanging God

Lays the foundation for my hope

In oaths, and promises, and blood."

MAY God help us to properly come before "the throne of grace." Amen.

(*A sermon on November 19, 1871, at the Metropolitan Tabernacle, Newington*).

Study Guide

This is a beautiful chapter that deals with the very aspect of coming to God, not under judgment, but in grace. Spurgeon's ability to unfold and unpack a very short phrase shows his skill as a teacher. Once we come to a place where we really understand how we come to God with our prayers, we can do so in freedom, and in that, find favor and honor with Him.

Working through these questions may lead you to ask other questions, or even reveal more aspects that you want to understand better. Sharing them with others is good; finding someone you trust, respect, and can guide you further is the best way to grow in your spiritual walk.

1. What do you understand about God sitting on the throne? Read Psalm 11:4 and Matthew 23:22.
2. Spurgeon admits that he worries we don't come before God's throne in the right attitude. He asks the Holy Spirit to help us. Do you need help in this regard?
3. Does grace change the way we come to God the King of kings?
4. When the phrase 'grace personified' is used, what does it mean? Read John 1:14-17.
5. Interestingly, Spurgeon looks at each aspect individually: Throne, grace, enthroned. Does your understanding of these change at all or emphasize the meaning when we read Hebrews 4:16 as a whole?
6. When it comes to prayer, what does this mean?

6

BRIEF, SILENT PRAYER

"So I prayed to the God of heaven."
Nehemiah 2:4

As we can see when we read the full passage that our key verse comes from, Nehemiah asked about the state of the city of Jerusalem, and the answer he received saddened him. *"Why should not my face be sad,"* he says, *"when the city, the place of my fathers' graves, lies in ruins, and its gates have been destroyed by fire?"* (Neh 2:3). It was too much for him to imagine it as a ruined heap—that city which was once beautiful and the joy of the whole earth. Taking it to heart, he did not begin to speak to other people about what they would do, nor did he draw up a wonderful scheme about what might be done if thousands of people joined in the plan, but it occurred to him that he would do something himself.

This is the way that practical people start something. The unpractical will plan, arrange, and speculate about what could be done, but the genuine, detailed lover of Zion puts this question to himself—"What can you do? Nehemiah, what can you do yourself? Come, it has to be done, and you are the man that has to do it—at least, to do your share. What can you do?" He decided to set apart a time for prayer. It stayed on his mind for nearly four months. Day and night Jerusalem seemed to be written on his heart as if the name was painted on his eyes. He could only see Jerusalem. When he slept, he dreamed about Jerusalem. When he woke, the first thought was "Poor Jerusalem!" and before he fell asleep again, his evening prayer was for the ruined walls of Jerusalem.

The person with only one vision and goal is a scary person, and when one single passion has absorbed their entire being, something is sure to come of it. You can depend on that. The desire of their heart will develop into some open demonstration, especially if they talk the matter over with God in prayer. Something did come of this. Before long, Nehemiah had an opportunity. Christians, if you want to serve God and cannot find the right occasion, wait in prayer and your opportunity will break on your path like sunlight.

No true and courageous heart has ever failed to find its place somewhere or other in His service. Every diligent worker is needed in some part of His vineyard. You may have to wait, you may seem as if you stood not doing anything for a while, because the Master would not use you, but wait there in prayer with your heart bubbling with purpose, and your chance will come. The right time will require someone, and if you are ready, you, as that someone, will not be without your right time.

God sent Nehemiah an opportunity. That opportunity came, even though it was not in a way that he could have expected. It came through his own sorrow. The matter of Jerusalem filled his mind until he began to look very unhappy. I am not sure if others saw it, but the king that he served noticed the distress on his cupbearer's face, and said to him, *"Why is your face sad, seeing you are not sick? This is nothing but sadness of the heart"* (Neh 2:2).

Nehemiah didn't know that his prayer was preparing this occasion for him. The prayer had been writing itself upon his face. His fasting was marking his features, and even though he didn't know it, he was preparing the opportunity for himself when he went in before the king. But we can see that when the opportunity did come, there was a problem because he says, *"Then I was very much afraid"* (Neh 2:2)

Maybe you want to serve God, and you want to be busy. Perhaps you don't know what that work involves. It's not all pleasure. Maybe you are desperate for the battle, young soldier, but you have not smelled the gunpowder yet. When you have been in a battle and have had a few cuts or a bullet or two have pierced you, you might not feel quite so eager for the battlefield. But the courageous person puts those things aside and is ready to serve his country or his king, and so the courageous Christian puts all difficulty aside and is ready to serve his comrades and his God, whatever it may cost.

What if I should be very much afraid? God, let it be that way if, through it, there will be an opportunity to seek and to secure the welfare of Jerusalem for Your servant, who longs to promote it with all his heart.

This leads us to where we find Nehemiah at the point of our key verse. The king, Artaxerxes, has asked him why he was sad, and he had an opportunity to tell him that the city of his fathers' was in ruin. So, the king asks him what he really wants. The way he asks the question seems to imply that he means to help him. It's surprising then, that, instead of immediately answering the king, an incident occurs, a fact is related. Though Nehemiah had been praying and fasting, this little parenthesis happens—"*So I prayed to the God of heaven.*"

The picture I have painted leads up to this parenthesis. In this prayer, I want us to learn something. There are three thoughts that I intend to look at in detail: The fact that Nehemiah prayed at that moment, the manner of his prayer, and the kind of prayer he used.

Nehemiah Prays

The fact that Nehemiah prayed at this moment demands our attention.

He had been asked a question by his king. In our minds, the proper thing would be to answer it. Not so. Before Nehemiah answered, he prayed to the God of heaven. I am not sure the king noticed the pause. Maybe the interval was not long enough to be noticed, but it was long enough for God to notice it—long enough for Nehemiah to have sought and have found guidance from God on how to answer the king. Are you surprised to find a man of God taking time to pray to God between a question and an answer? Yet Nehemiah found that time. We are amazed that he prayed because he was so evidently worried in his mind; as we have seen, he was very afraid. When you are anxious and aggravated you might forget to pray.

Maybe some of us use it as a valid excuse for skipping our normal time of devotion. At least, if anyone had said to you, "You did not pray when you were going through that episode," you could have replied, "How could I? There was a question that I was obliged to answer. I dared not hesitate. It was a king that asked it. I was in a state of confusion. I really was so distressed and terrified that I was not in control of my emotions. I hardly knew what I did. If I did not pray, surely that can be excused. I was in a state of panic."

Nehemiah, however, felt that if he was panicked, it was a reason for praying, not for forgetting to pray. So habitually was he in communion with God that as soon as he found himself in a dilemma, he turned to God, just as the dove would fly to hide in the clefts of the rock.

His prayer was even more remarkable because he must have felt very eager about his vision and goal. The king asks him what he wants, and his whole heart is set on building up Jerusalem. Are you not surprised that he did not immediately say, "Oh king, live forever. I long to build up Jerusalem's walls. Give me all the help you can"? But, as eager as he was to take hold of his goal, he keeps his hand back until he prayed to the God of heaven. I admire him. I also want to imitate him.

I wish every Christian's heart might have as much holy caution to stop us rushing in too soon. It was George Herbert who said, "Prayers and provender hinder no man's journey." Certainly, when the desire of our heart is right before us, we are anxious to grab it, but we will catch the bird in the bush if we wait quietly, lift our heart and pray to the God of heaven.

It's even more surprising that Nehemiah should have prayed at that moment because he had been already praying for the past three or four months about the same matter. Some of us would have said, "That is the thing I have been praying for, now all I have to do is to take it and use it. Why pray more? After all, my midnight tears and daily cries, and fasting before God, surely, at last, the answer has come. What else must be done but to take the good that God provides me and rejoice in it?" But, you will always find that the person who has prayed much is the person who will pray even more. *"For to the one who has, more will be given, and he will have an abundance"* (Matt 13:12). If you know the sweet art of prayer, you are the person that will be often engaged in it. If you are familiar with the mercy seat you will constantly visit it—

"For who that knows the power of prayer

But wishes to be often there?"

. . .

Although Nehemiah had been praying all this time, he still needed to offer another request. *"So I prayed to the God of heaven."*

There is one more thing worth looking at: He was in a king's palace and in the palace of a heathen king too, and he was in the very act of giving the cup of wine to the king. He was doing his job in the court, among the glare of lamps and the glitter of gold and silver, in the midst of princes and nobles of the kingdom. Even if it were a private function with only the king and queen, people can be so impressed with the responsibility of their high position in those occasions, that they forget prayer. But this devoted Israelite, at such a time and in such a place, when he stands before the king to give him the golden goblet, does not answer the king's question until he has first prayed to the God of heaven.

The Manner of Prayer

There is much more we can say, but let's move to look at the manner of his prayer.

This was what we call a brief prayer—prayer that throws a dart and then it is done. It was not the prayer which stands knocking at mercy's door—knock, knock, knock, but it was the concentration of many knocks in one. It was started and completed with one stroke. I see this brief, quick prayer as one of the very best forms of prayer.

Notice how short it must have been. It was introduced—slipped in—sandwiched in—between the king's question and Nehemiah's answer. And as I have already said, I don't think it took up any time at all—hardly a second. The king probably never observed any pause or hesitation, because Nehemiah was in such a panic at the question that I am sure he didn't allow any doubt to appear, but the prayer must have been offered like an electric flash, very quickly indeed.

In certain times of excitement, it is amazing how much the mind gets through in a short time. Maybe you have dreamed while you slept, and your dream felt as though it was for an hour or two at the very least, yet it's possible that all dreaming is done at the moment you wake up. You never dreamed at all when you were asleep, it was just in that instant when you woke up that everything went through your mind. Drowning men, when rescued and recovered, have said that while they were sinking they saw the whole of their lives pass before them in a few seconds. So, the mind must be capable of accomplishing lots in a brief space of time. Nehemiah's prayer was made in the wink of an eye, it was done intuitively, and it was a prayer that succeeded with God.

We also know that it must have been a silent prayer, and not just silent in terms of sound, but silent in the heart—perfectly secret. Artaxerxes never knew that Nehemiah prayed, even though he stood probably less than a few meters from him. He didn't even move his lips as Hannah did, nor did he even close his eyes, but the prayer was offered only to God. In the inner room of the temple—in the holy of holies of his own secret heart—there he prayed.

The prayer was short and silent. It was a prayer on the spot. He did not go to his room as Daniel did, and opened the window. Daniel was correct, but this was a different occasion. Nehemiah would not have been allowed to leave his palace duties at that moment. He didn't even turn his face to the wall or look for a corner of the apartment. No, but there and then, with the cup in his hand, he prayed to the God of heaven, and then answered the king's question.

I do not doubt the way the verse is written, that it was a very intense and direct prayer. He says, *"So I prayed to the God of heaven."* That was Nehemiah's favorite name for God—the God of heaven. He knew whom he was praying to. He did not draw a bow and shoot his prayers randomly, but he prayed to the God of heaven—a true, straight prayer to God for the thing he wanted, and his prayer sped, even though it probably took less than a second to say.

It was a remarkable kind of prayer. I know this because Nehemiah never forgot that he prayed it. I have prayed hundreds of times, thousands of times, and don't remember the occasion that prompted or the emotions that excited me, but there are one or two prayers in my life that I can never forget. I have not written them down in a diary, but I remember when I prayed, because the time was so special and the prayer was so intense, and the answer to it was so remarkable.

Now, Nehemiah's prayer was never erased from his memory, and when these words of history were recorded, he wrote that down, *"So I prayed to the God of heaven."* It was such a small prayer pushed in between a question and an answer, a fragment of devotion, and yet so important that we find it in a historical document as a part of the history of the restitution and rebuilding of the city of Jerusalem, and a link in the circumstances which led up to that event of the most important character. Nehemiah felt it was important, and so he records the words: *"So I prayed to the God of heaven."*

The Style of Praying

Let us look at the third aspect, which is Nehemiah's excellent style of praying.

This part is aimed mainly at Christians, those that have faith in God. I beg you and ask you to always use this method of brief, silent prayer. And I hope that those who have never prayed before would offer a brief, silent prayer to the God of heaven before we are finished—that a short but urgent request might go up, like the one the tax collector in the temple prayed—*"God, be merciful to me, a sinner"* (Luke 18:13).

To deal with this matter practically, the duty and privilege of every Christian is to have set times of prayer. I cannot understand how a person can keep up a godly life unless they regularly take time out for prayer, at least every morning and evening. Daniel prayed three times a day, and David says, *"Seven times a day I praise you"* (Psalm 119:164). It is good for your heart, good for your memory, good for your moral consistency that you should schedule in certain portions of time and say, "These belong to God. I will do business with God at this time, and try to be as punctual with Him as if I had made an engagement to meet a friend."

When Sir Thomas Abney was Lord Mayor of London, the formal banquet that was being held, became an issue for him, because he always prayed with his family at a certain time, which coincided with the time of the banquet. The difficulty was how to quit the banquet to keep up his family devotion, but it was so important to him that he left his place at the meal, saying to a person nearby that he had a special engagement with a dear friend that he must keep. And he did keep it, and came back to his place when he had finished—none of those at the banquet had any idea what he had done, but he was in a better place for observing his routine habit of worship.

Mrs. Rowe used to say that when her time came for prayer she would not give it up if the apostle Paul was preaching. "No," she said, "if all the twelve apostles were there, and could be heard at no other time, she would not leave her prayer room when the time came round." Well, I don't think that my own standards would go quite as far as that because if I had the opportunity of hearing the apostle at the time when I usually pray, and could not hear him at any other time, I would postpone my prayer to hear the sermon. I don't think it would be improper at all, it would show a little shrewd sense. Yet, as a general principle, it is good to be punctual and diligent in respect to your private as well as your public prayers. Don't be negligent, but vigilant; never be careless, but always regular in keeping your appointed times of prayer.

But now, having stressed the importance of habitual devotion, I want to emphasize the value of another sort of prayer—the short, brief, quick, frequent prayers like the one we saw Nehemiah use. And I recommend this because it is no obstacle to engagements and does not take up much time.

You may be measuring off your curtains, or weighing your groceries, or you may be drawing up an account, and between the items, you may say, "Lord, help me." You may breathe a prayer to heaven and say, "Lord, keep me." It will take no time.

It's one great advantage to people who are so busy at work that these kinds of prayers won't stop them from attending to the business they have to do in the slightest. It doesn't require you to go to a particular place. You can stand where you are, ride in a cab, walk along the streets, be at the bottom of the factory, or in the office, and still pray these prayers just as well. No altar, no church, no so-called sacred place is needed, but wherever you are, just a little prayer like that will reach the ear of God, and win a blessing. Such a prayer can be offered anywhere, under any circumstances.

I don't know what condition a person could be in that they might not offer this kind of prayer. On the land or the sea, in sickness or health, in times of losses or gains, great reverses or good returns, the heart can still breathe in short, quick sentences to God. The advantage of this way of praying is that you can pray often and always. If you are looking to have a longer prayer of fifteen minutes you might not be able to spare the time, but if it's only fifteen seconds, then you can do it again and again and again—a hundred times a day. The habit of prayer is blessed, but the spirit of prayer is better, and the spirit of prayer is the mother of these brief silent prayers; that's why I like them because she is a plentiful mother. Many times in a day we can speak with the Lord our God.

This type of prayer can be incited by any kind of surrounding. I remember a poor man once paid me a compliment that I really valued at the time. He was lying in a hospital, and when I came to see him, he said, "I heard you for some years, and now whatever I look at seems to remind me of something or other that you said, and it comes back to me as fresh as when I first heard it." The person that knows how to pray brief, silent prayers will find everything about him as an encouragement or help into the sacred habit.

Is it a beautiful landscape? Then say, "Blessed be God who has poured these treasures of shapes and colors into the world, to create a wonderful view and bring joy to the heart." Are you in dull darkness, and is it a foggy day? Then you can say, "Lighten my darkness, O Lord." Are you in the midst of company? You will be reminded to pray, "Lord, keep the door of my lips." Are you alone? Then you can say, "Let me not be alone, but You be with me, Father."

Dressing into your clothes, eating breakfast in the morning, going to work, walking on the street, opening your assignments, closing work for the day—everything can suggest a prayer as those I am trying to describe if you are in the right frame of mind for offering it.

These prayers are commendable because they are truly spiritual. Wordy prayers can also be windy prayers. There is a lot of praying by the book that is not recommended as it is empty. The benefit of a French-language guide for anyone traveling in France without a knowledge of the language is very limited. A book of prayers will do the same for a poor person who does not know how to ask their heavenly Father for something that they need. A manual, a handbook? Pray with your heart, not with your hands. Or, if you want to lift your hands in prayer, let them be your own hands, not another man's. The prayers that come leaping out of the heart—the gust of strong emotion, passionate desire, lively faith—these are truly spiritual, and God won't accept any prayers but spiritual prayers.

This kind of prayer is also free from the corrupt motive of being said in order to please others. They cannot say that the secret, brief, silent prayers of our heart are presented to receive our own praise, for no one knows that we are praying at all, so I do recommend this kind of prayer to you and hope that you may grow in it.

There have been hypocrites that have prayed for hours. I don't doubt that there are hypocrites who have as many regular devotions as the angels bow before the throne of God, and yet there is no life, no spirit, no acceptance in their pretending. But those that pray brief silent prayers—whose heart talks with God—that person is not a hypocrite. There is a reality, and force, and life about it. If I see sparks come out of a chimney, I know there is a fire inside somewhere, and brief silent prayers are like the sparks that fly from a heart that is filled with burning coals of love to Jesus Christ.

Brief, silent prayers are very useful to us. Often they check us. Bad-tempered people, if you prayed just before you said some angry expressions from your mouth, then most times you would not say those offensive words at all. Once, they advised a woman to take a glass of water and put some of it in her mouth and hold it there for five minutes before she scolded her husband. It sounds like a very good recipe, but instead of practicing that little trick, if she just breathed a short prayer to God, it would certainly be more effective, and far more biblical.

I can recommend it as a valuable method for those in a rush and those who are moody, for all those who are quick to take offense and slow to forgive insults or injuries. In business, when you are about to close a deal that you are not completely sure of or have second thoughts about, a prayer like, "Guide me, Lord" can often keep you from doing something that you will later regret.

The habit of offering these brief prayers will also keep a check on your confidence in yourself. It will show your dependence on God. It will keep you from becoming worldly. It will be like a sweet perfume burned in your heart to keep out the fever of the world. I can strongly recommend these short, sweet, blessed prayers. May the Holy Spirit give them to you!

These prayers are not just good for our character and spiritual growth, they actually bring us blessings from heaven. Brief silent prayers, as in the case of Eliezer, the servant of Abraham, as in the case of Jacob when he said even in death, *"I wait for your salvation, O Lord"* (Gen 49:18)—prayers like the ones Moses offered when we do not read that he prayed at all, and yet God asked him why he was crying to Him, and brief, silent prayers such as David often said, these were all successful with the Most High. So use them and grow in them, because God loves to encourage and to answer them.

I could carry on recommending brief prayer, but I will only add one more thing in its favor. I believe it is very suitable for certain people with strange characters who cannot pray for a long time to save their lives. Their minds are quick. Time is not an issue in this regard, God does not hear us because of the length of our prayer, but because of the sincerity of it. Prayer is not to be measured by the meter, nor weighed by the pound. It is the might and force of it—the truth and reality of it—the energy and the intensity of it. Anyone who's somehow incapacitated in their brain or slow in thinking, and can't use many words, or continue to think of one thing for very long, it should be an encouragement that brief prayers are acceptable.

And it may be that your body is in a condition in which you cannot pray any other way. A headache, like those that some people frequently get and are a major issue in their lives—a state which the doctor can explain to you—might prevent the mind from concentrating on one subject for very long. Then it is refreshing to be able to address yourself to God in short, quick sentences, the soul being all on fire, again and again, and again—fifty or a hundred times a day. This is a wonderful form of praying.

Now, I conclude by mentioning a few of the times when I think we should resort to this practice of brief, silent prayer. Mr. Rowland Hill was a remarkable man for the depth of his character and godliness, but when I asked for his study, even though I asked the question quite directly, I did not get a satisfactory reply. After a while, the minister said, "The fact is, we never found any. Mr. Hill used to study in the garden, in the parlor, in the bedroom, in the streets, in the woods, anywhere." I asked where he went off to pray and be alone. They said they supposed it was in his room, but that he was always praying—that it did not matter where he was, the old man was always praying. It seemed as if his whole life, though he spent it among people doing good, was done in continual prayer.

There is another story of Mr. Hill being in Walworth at the chapel where Paul Turquand is now the pastor, and of being seen in the aisles after everybody was gone, while he was waiting for his lift to come. There was the old man hobbling up and down the aisles, and as someone listened, he heard him singing to himself—

"And when I shall die, receive me I'll cry,

For Jesus has loved me, I cannot tell why;

But this thing I find, we two are so joined,

He won't be in heaven and leave me behind."

AND WITH SUCH RHYMES, songs, and gracious words, he would spend every moment of his life. He was known to stand in the Blackfriars' road with his hands behind his back, looking in a shop window, and if you listened, you would have heard him breathing out his heart before God. He had got into a constant state of prayer. I believe it is the best condition a person can be in—praying always, praying without ceasing, always drawing near to God with these brief prayers.

Let me mention a few moments when these kinds of prayers are most useful. Whenever something good happens to you, say, "Lord, make this a real blessing to me." Don't shout out like other people, "Am I not a lucky person?" but say, "Lord, give me more grace, and more gratitude, now that You bless me so much." When you have got any strenuous task or business to see to, don't touch it until you have breathed your heart out in a short prayer. When you have difficulty before you, and you are seriously worried when the business has got into a tangle or a confession that you can't unravel or set right, breathe a prayer. It doesn't need to occupy a minute, but it is wonderful how many traps come loose after just a word of prayer.

Are your children behaving badly or giving you trouble? Does it seem as if your patience is almost worn out with the worry and pestering? Time for a brief prayer. You will manage them all the better, and you will put up with their naughty attitudes more quietly. At least your own mind will be less ruffled. Do you think that there is a temptation before you? Do you suspect that somebody is plotting against you? Time for a prayer, *"Lead me on a level path because of my enemies"* (Psalm 27:11). Are you at work in the office, or in a shop, or a warehouse, where disgusting conversation and blasphemies hurt your ears? Time for a short prayer. Have you noticed some sin that grieves you? Let it bring you to prayer. These things should remind you to pray.

I believe the devil would not let people swear so much if Christians prayed every time they heard someone cursing. He would then see it does not pay. Their blasphemies would become quiet if they knew it provoked us to pray. Do you feel your own heart going off the lines? Does sin begin to fascinate you? Time for a prayer—a warm, sincere, passionate cry, "Lord, hold you me up!" Did you see something with your eye, and did that eye infect your heart? Do you feel as if you're in a place where you say, *"my feet had almost stumbled, my steps had nearly slipped"* (Psalm 73:2)? Time for a prayer—"Hold me, Lord, by my right hand." Has something quite unexpected happened? Has a friend treated you badly? Then, like David, say, *"O Lord, please turn the counsel of Ahithophel into foolishness"* (2 Sam 15:31). Breathe a prayer now.

Are you keen to do something good? Be sure to pray about it. Do you want to speak to that young person about their soul as they go out of the church tonight? Pray first. Do you want to talk to the students in your class or write them a letter about their spiritual well-being? Pray over every line.

It's always good to be praying while you are talking about Jesus. I always find I can preach better if I can pray while I am preaching. And the mind is remarkable in what it can do. It can be praying while it is studying, it can be looking up to God while it is talking to a person, and there can be one hand held up to receive supplies from God while the other hand is dealing out the same supplies which He is pleased to give. Pray as long as you live. Pray when you are in great pain, the sharper the hurt then the more urgent and persistent your cry to God should be. And when the shadow of death comes around you, and you have strange feelings or a chill on you, and you can tell that you are near the journey's end, then pray. That is a time for a brief prayer. Short and quick prayers like this—"Don't hide Your face from me, O Lord," or "Don't be far from me, O God," will suit the moment. *"Lord Jesus, receive my spirit"* (Acts 7:59) were the thrilling words of Stephen at his very end, and *"Father, into your hands I commit my spirit!"* (Luke 23:46) were the words that Jesus said just before He bowed His head and died. You would do well to copy Him.

These thoughts and advice are exclusively aimed at those who are already Christians that you may ask, "Isn't there anything to be said about those not yet born again?" If they hear this same advice, it can also be used by them for their own benefit. But let me say this as clearly as possible: Even though you are not yet saved, you must not say, "I can't pray." If prayer is so simple, what excuse can you have for not trying it? It doesn't need any measure of time. Prayers like these will be heard by God, and you all have the ability and opportunity to think and to express them, even if you only have a small beginner's faith in God that believes *"that he exists and that he rewards those who seek him"* (Heb 11:6).

Cornelius probably got as far as this, when he was rebuked by the angel to send for Peter, who preached to him peace by Jesus Christ so that he was born again. Is there such a strange being in the church as a man or woman that never prays? How shall I disagree with you? Maybe I can steal a passage from Tennyson who, though he has contributed nothing to our hymn books, says something that suits my purpose, and is so pleasant to hear, that I like to quote it—

"More things are accomplished by prayer

Than this world dreams of. Why let your voice

Rise like a fountain, flowing night and day:

For what are men better than sheep or goats,

That nourish a blind life within the brain,

If knowing God, they lift not hands of prayer,

Both for themselves and those who call them friend?

For so the whole round world is every way

Bound by gold chains about the feet of God."

I DON'T THINK there is a person who never prays, because people generally pray to somebody or other. The person that never prays to God the prayers he should, prays to God those prayers that he should not. It is a terrible thing when a man asks God to damn him, and yet there are people that do that. Suppose He heard you, He is a prayer-hearing God. If anyone of you swears a lot, I would like to put this matter clearly to you.

If the Almighty heard you, and you were struck blind and dumb while you were saying your wild words, how would you handle the sudden judgment on your what you said? If some of those prayers of yours were answered for yourself, and some that you have said in the heat of the moment about your wife and your child, were fulfilled to their injury and your amusement, what an awful thing it would be! Well, God does answer prayer, and one of these days He may answer your prayers to your shame and everlasting confusion.

It would be good before we finish for you to pray, "Lord, have mercy upon me; Lord, save me; Lord, change my heart; Lord, help me to believe in Jesus; Lord, open my eyes to the precious blood of Jesus; Lord, save me now." Won't every one of you breathe such a prayer as that? May the Holy Spirit lead you to do so, and if you begin to pray correctly, I am convinced that you will never stop, because there is something that holds the heart in real prayer. Pretend, mock prayers—what is the good of them? But a real heart pleading—the soul talking with God—when it begins, it will never cease. You will have to pray until you exchange prayer for praise, and go from the mercy seat below to the throne of God above.

May God bless you all, all of you—all who are with me in Jesus, and all those whose salvation I long for. God bless you all and everyone, for our Redeemer's sake. Amen.

(A sermon on September 9, 1877, at the Metropolitan Tabernacle, Newington).

Study Guide

Having worked through the whole book, you may find that you want to revisit a certain chapter. Spurgeon's writings are so full of new ways to see things or challenging sentences and ideas that often you have to reread portions again and again just to digest them properly.

In this chapter, we find Spurgeon at his practical best; giving us a method of praying that is not only possible to fit into our busy schedules but is also just as effective.

1. It is made clear that Daniel and Hannah's long times of prayer were correct, so why is Nehemiah's short one just as worthy?
2. Set times of prayer as important, according to Spurgeon. Do you find these easy to stick to in your life?
3. The examples of people who prioritized prayer above everything else are very challenging. In your own life, where does prayer rank?
4. Does this style of brief, silent prayers line up with 1 Thessalonians 5:17?
5. What area of your prayer life needs attention?

Having worked through these questions, you may want to do some further reading on prayer. Some good books by solid, reputable writers are:

- The Hidden Life of Prayer - David M. McIntyre
- A Call to Prayer - J.C. Ryle
- How to Pray Effectively - R.A. Torrey

ABOUT C. H. SPURGEON

Charles Haddon Spurgeon is one of the more renowned Christian writers and preachers of the late 19th century and is fondly known as the "Prince of Preachers."

Born in Essex on 19 June 1834, Spurgeon grew up in a family of clerics. He never had the privilege of a good education, attending only a few local schools and not gaining any kind of university degree. Although he was not a fan of formal schooling, he loved books and learning and had a personal library of over 12,000 books.

At the age of 15, a snowstorm forced him to take cover in a Methodist church while traveling, where he was born again. He was baptized a few days later and left the family denomination to join a Baptist church.

As a young teen, he began preaching, and his style and energy filled the pews until he was invited to New Park Street Chapel in London. Although only there on probation, the congregation voted for him to stay on. From there, he began traveling around the city; often preaching to thousands. His sharp memory allowed him to speak without being tied to notes, and he often acted out passages or stories during his sermons. With the popularity of his teaching, however, there also came criticism—something he lived with until he died.

Straight down the line, simple, and direct, people were either cut to the heart or incensed at his antics. "I am perhaps vulgar, but it is not intentional, save that I must and will make people listen. My firm conviction is that we have had enough polite preachers," he said in response.

Apart from his prolific preaching and writing, he found time to open an orphanage as well as a Pastor's College in 1855. From 1861, he saw the move of his congregation into the Metropolitan Tabernacle that could seat 5,000. At that time, it was the largest church in the world. Relying on the Bible as the basis for his arguments, he challenged other denominations on their belief in infant baptism and on the issue of slavery. Outspoken, he never backed down.

At the age of 37 his doctors advised him to rest, and so he took time off in France where he received many visitors such as George Muller. However, his health never regained properly and in 1891, he was forced to stop all his public duties. In February of the following year, he passed away, and 800 extra policemen were brought in to contain the massive crowds that gathered for his funeral.

Although he challenged many on their beliefs according to doctrine and denomination, he always had one goal, summed up in his own words, "If I am asked what is my creed, I reply, 'It is Jesus Christ.'"

www.ingramcontent.com/pod-product-compliance
Lightning Source LLC
LaVergne TN
LVHW010218070526
838199LV00062B/4644